If the
TABLE
Could
TALK

A TASTE of CELEBRATIONS

If the
TABLE
Could
TALK

A TASTE of CELEBRATIONS

Alyssa Alia

Recipes and Food Styling by Alyssa Alia
Photographs by Al Owens

MALANGA PUBLISHING

If the Table Could Talk...what would it say?

*Alyssa Alia, a prominent New York area food stylist and mother of two,
shares her most cherished recipes from her table to yours.*

*Captured by the menus she's saved from decades of home celebrations,
you'll find within these pages a treasure trove of well-loved family recipes -
delectable, fun, easy-to-prepare and filled with joy! These recipes, developed
and prepared lovingly by Alyssa over many years, are presented here with
time-saving tips, make-ahead tricks, decorating ideas and hints for
how to make every gathering you host a success.*

*Beautiful photography brings each recipe in this cookbook to life,
a testament to Alyssa's talent as a food stylist.*

*So, sit back and enjoy Alyssa's menus, her food journal through time,
and let it inspire you to create your own food memories with family and friends!*

Prop Styling and Photo Art Direction by
Michele Jerry of Limoncello Productions
Prop Styling for Photograph on page 112 by Deb Ruggieri, Prop That

Book Design and Art Direction by
Nancy Hourihan of Red Relish Creative
Lisa Curran of Creative Designory

Managing Editor: Marisa Malanga
Assistant Copy Editors: Maria Malanga, Donna Saiewitz
and Jack Hourihan

Food Styling Assistants: Maria Malanga, Marisa Malanga,
Christopher McMahon, Geovanna Colindres, Donna Saiewitz
and Tracy McKenna

Published and Produced by Malanga Publishing/
Triple A Productions, LLC

ISBN 978-0-9981313-4-4
First Edition

www.alyssaalia.com

@Alyssa Alia Food Stylist

@alyssaalia

alyssa alia food stylist

Alyssa Alia

Alyssa Alia

*"For my joy, my bliss,
my most precious blessings -
my daughters, Maria & Marisa"
xoxo*

contents

A Taste of Celebrations

Foreword

Alyssa is a dear friend and colleague. She is also a wife, a mother, sister, aunt, and good friend to a small group of her immediate and extended family—which is a group of hundreds, maybe even thousands of people. Everyone loves Alyssa!

Alyssa is a world-class food stylist. I met her many years ago on a photo shoot, and we have not stopped working together since.

If the Table Could Talk is the result of the combined efforts of some truly amazing people. It was a great privilege to be part of the creative team who produced the images that feature Alyssa's recipes. For the creative team, each recipe is a living short story from Alyssa's life. For you who may be seeing this book for the first time, the recipes are a chance to create new memories.

Photography has defined my life, not simply because of the magic it makes me feel, but more importantly because of the people it has connected me with throughout my career. I love the people I work with and that's what this book is all about, love! Love of food and the people to whom we express that love through cooking, sharing meals and creating new memories.

Alyssa's capacity for love is amazing. Her book is the result of a lifetime of memories that all evolved around food as an expression of that love. Each recipe Alyssa prepared for the photography in this book prompted a new story that she shared as we set up for each photo. A vivid and beautiful history of each recipe was passed on to us as Alyssa worked. Her words were unscripted and spontaneous, and quite beautiful to hear. We heard so many stories — cooking with her mother when she was a child, baking with her neighbor as a little girl, her dad's favorites, and her husband Tommy's favorites, as well as newer cooking memories created with her daughters. In addition to the recipes, each well-used item in Alyssa's kitchen arsenal had its own story connected to her rich history. Every rolling pin, cake pan, and cutting board was special to her because of its legacy or a memory she had of using it with a family member or friend.

We produced the photography for this book at Alyssa's home rather than at a studio. At first it just made logistical sense, but I quickly realized we were in the perfect setting to create the photos because Alyssa's home is where so much of the book's content was born. Alyssa's husband Tommy and their daughters, Maria and Marisa, were often on set as we worked, making the images feel right and authentic. They are all very special people.

Alyssa understands that preparing and sharing food allows us to spend meaningful time with people who matter to us. So, prepare these recipes the way they were created and preserved by Alyssa...with love!

Thank you, Alyssa, for this book and your endless optimism, support and encouragement.

Let's eat!

Al Owens / Photographer / July 2016

A Letter from Alyssa

If your table could talk, what would it tell you? In my life the most heartfelt loving memories were made when gathered around my family's table. Whether it be an everyday dinner with your children or a celebratory occasion, every moment that you gather and share food at the table brings people together. I wanted to recreate these memories by sharing recipes that were served around my table with love, throughout my life. I have said, so often, that eating and enjoying meals around the table reinforces the most precious memories of family and friends. The menus in this book are a lifelong autobiography, recorded memoir of milestone events and impromptu occasions at my table. My first menu on record was celebrating my engagement to my husband. I invited my future in-laws over my parents' house and hand wrote my menu in calligraphy. I still have that menu 30 years later. That first menu inspired me from then on to write menus for every event I cooked in my home. I must have 100s of them. My menus are a treasured journal through time. I am so thankful to reminisce and savor every recipe that was shared at my table with loved ones. Whether it was one of my daughters' 1st birthdays, my dad's 80th birthday or a simple summer gathering with friends on my patio to my children's backyard graduation parties, the memories will live on through these prized and tantalizing recipes.

I have been a lover of food and passionate about cooking since I was three years old. I have been a professional food stylist for over 30 years, so I have included delicious photographs throughout the book that I prepared and food styled for your enjoyment. My goal is to fulfill your cravings and desires through these irresistible photographs. I truly believe a picture captures 1,000 mouthwatering memories and it is my hope that these photographs entice you to try them all—to anticipate every bite.

I invite you to enjoy this sampling of recipes from my menus, that hold a special place in my heart. They are easy and fun, and most are even make-ahead. Many were inspired through family and holiday traditions, and others from friends, professional and personal. I have also included shopping and entertaining tips with time saving ideas and helpful tricks. Since my professional life is styling food in the most beautiful way it can be for the camera, I have also included easy garnish and serving suggestions to make your parties showstoppers with minimal fuss and ease.

But make me one promise before you begin—make these recipes your own! Change them to suit your family and yourself. If you do not care for arugula, use another green leaf. If you are not a nut person, eliminate them. There are no limits to the culinary arts and the beauty of sharing recipes is to make them your new creations. Redesign them for your needs and taste and make it a whole new food experience. Please use these recipes just simply as guides and make new memories around your table!

Thank you for this special opportunity to share my life-filled love of food along side you.

Keep your table talking!

En-JOY and cook just for the love it,

Alyssa xo

About The Author

I can still remember standing next to my grandmother, my Nana, with my chin-counter height, cutting the struffoli for Christmas at age four! I enjoyed every kitchen moment and became an essential assistant for all of my family's meals. Food prep became a culinary obsession and my family encouraged me to pursue my talents in the kitchen. My favorite Christmas gift was my first electric mixer at ten years old, a stainless Sunbeam Mixmaster. I was obsessed with this mixer and polished it every time I used it. I still have it to this day.

Growing up in an Italian household exposed me to cooking traditions, family Sunday dinners and healthy food preparation on a daily basis.

At 12 years old, I started baking with my neighbor, Mrs. Betty Ann Maryott, who could have been a successful pastry chef herself. Every cookie she made was picture perfect! She lovingly taught me after school, at her house, my first official cake decorating lessons. I began to cake decorate everything I could, starting my art skills and patience for perfect results with practice, practice, practice. Our next door neighbor, Mrs. Kovak, was an excellent Czechoslovakian baker. She taught me the meaning of technique and the importance of patience in pastry making. I couldn't wait to help and watch her make her homemade strudel pastry dough on Saturday afternoons.

At 16 years old, my Mom saw a help wanted sign in the window of a small gourmet store front called Cooktique in Tenafly, New Jersey, near where we lived in Closter. I applied and was hired as the owner's runner and assistant for two summers and on weekends during the school year. The owner, Silvia Lehrer, gave me my first opportunity to work in a professional culinary atmosphere and I was hooked the minute I walked into her store. She also had a small cooking school in the back of the store where she taught classic cooking classes. I was the shopper, prepper and food gopher while demonstrating the newest craze, the Cuisinart Food Processor! Here is where I learned one of my most valuable cooking lessons, especially to make stock, stock and more stock. She would also have guest chefs for a few weeks each summer to teach specialty classes and promote their first cookbooks. I was able to assist the renown French chef Jacques Pépin and the famous Italian chef noted for his extraordinary pasta making, Giuliano Bugialli. What a thrill and I didn't even know what celebrities they would become! I was just enamored by them - I was in cooking heaven. This was my passion and that is when I knew I wanted to pursue a career in food.

I also worked as a Friendly's waitress the last three years of high school. Here is where I learned my people skills as well as service skills. I believe every person should be a waiter or waitress at least once in their lifetime. It makes you appreciate all kinds of people and teaches you how to accommodate while making them feel happy, even if it's for a moment. People will appreciate your kindness and pass it on.

During that time in high school my dad encouraged me to write to the food editors of national magazines to ask them how to pursue a career in the culinary arts. This was life-changing advice as many of them wrote back with college choices and even class suggestions. I was accepted to Cornell University and obtained a bachelors degree in nutritional sciences but I still was longing for more culinary training.

For two college summers, my Dad also thought I should apply as an intern at the Lipton Company, now known as Unilever, where I was asked to work in the food science department. They introduced me to the Lipton Test Kitchens down the hall. This department developed and tested recipes for their food products and, again, I realized I needed to be in a kitchen environment. After graduating from Cornell, I was hired as a Test Kitchen Home Economist at Lipton and worked there for three years. I learned so much about the corporate food industry but I still longed for more advanced culinary training. I decided to leave Lipton and enrolled into a full time culinary chef program at the New York Restaurant School in New York City. I fell into my heaven and loved the training every day in my chef whites. I graduated with a chef certification with honors. Soon after, the school sponsored students for some extra training at Le Cordon Bleu, France, my dream school!

After returning from Europe, I applied to many food magazines in New York City. One of the food editors, Jean Voltz, remembered my high school letter and hired me several times as a freelancer. I continued to freelance, over three years, for numerous publications. It was here where I performed more recipe development but then I would also be asked to go into the photography studio to food style the recipes for the camera. Everything started to click together for me. My food science training at Cornell, my culinary passion, love of food art, and then my professional culinary training - it was the perfect blend to become a professional food stylist. I continue to freelance as a food stylist presently. I have food styled over the years for many major food companies as well as magazines, for print, packaging, film, advertising, social media and video applications. It has been a whirlwind career path but I have loved every minute of it. This profession trained me to create on the spot, keep my cooking skills sharp, prepare efficiently and therefore perform quickly and effortlessly with patience and kindness at every job. Food styling is almost like performing on stage, it's live and you are as good as your last job. There is no room for mistakes so practice and preparation are key. Your food is your musical art while your client is your audience and ultimate critic. You want the best reviews every time.

All my years of experience and polished culinary skills helped me to be efficient in my home kitchen for entertaining as well as feed my family in a moment's notice. As a working mother of two, I had a demanding career but I used honed skills to my advantage in every cooking event that crossed my kitchen.

This book is a tribute to my life learning that made me not only the professional I am today in my craft but the excited home cook who just loves to be in the kitchen, everyday, just for the love of it!

brunch

Time for Brunch

Brie En Croute *with* Raspberry and Almonds

Crab and Spinach Dip

Broccoli and Cheddar Quiche *with* Puffed Pastry Crust

Baked French Toast *with* Bananas Foster Topping

Maple Glazed Bacon Wrapped Breadsticks

Potato and Egg Strata *with* Fontina, Swiss and Mozzarella

Berry-ful Lemony Scones

Marisa's Triple Threat Berry Muffins

Super Huge Crumb Cake

Lemon Curd Tarts

Toasted Coconut, Almond and Chocolate Cake

Brie En Croute *with* Raspberry and Almonds

Makes 12 Servings

Preheat oven to 400°F.

16 phyllo sheets
½ cup (1 stick) butter, melted

} Unroll sheets on dampened kitchen towel, and lightly brush top sheet with some of the butter.

1 round (13 ounces) brie

} Place in center of sheet.
Slice in half horizontally.

½ cup raspberry preserves or jam*
½ cup toasted, sliced almonds*

} Spread on first half of brie. Top with second half of brie like a sandwich.

Brushing each sheet of phyllo with butter, wrap six phyllo sheets around brie.

Place wrapped brie on lightly greased baking sheet, seam side down.

Continue to lightly brush each phyllo sheet with butter, carefully placing on top of wrapped brie and gathering them at the top like a flower.
Brush with any remaining butter.

Bake for 20 minutes or until lightly golden.
Serve with assorted cut fruit and crackers.

TIPS:

Can substitute phyllo sheets with 2 frozen puff pastry sheets. Unfold one defrosted puff pastry sheet and wrap brie as above. Use second sheet to cut and decorate as you like. Brush with egg yolk mixed with 1 tablespoon water and brush pastry before baking. Bake according to package directions.

Can be assembled and chilled one day ahead.

Substitute ½ cup apricot preserves mixed with 1 tablespoon whole grain mustard or horseradish for extra zestiness.

Substitute ½ cup fig jam with 2 strips cooked and crumbled bacon and 2 tablespoons bleu cheese or Gorgonzola.

Substitute ½ cup pesto with 2 tablespoons chopped sun-dried tomatoes and 2 tablespoons toasted pignoli nuts.

Substitute ½ cup strawberry preserves, 2 tablespoons chopped dried cranberries and 2 tablespoons chopped pecans.

This filling is delicious, but you can use any desired filling combination. Use your favorite jams or preserves!

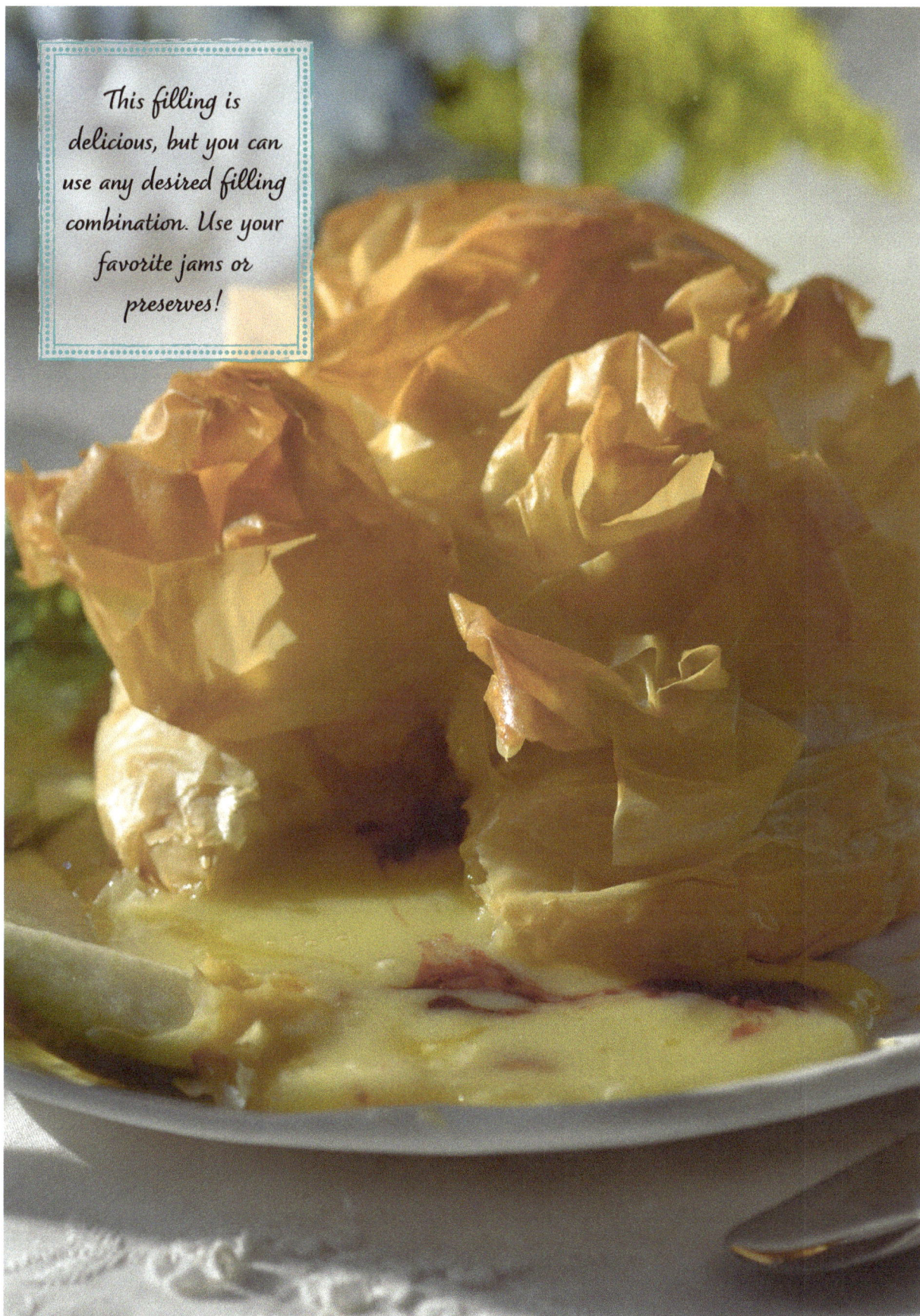

Crab and Spinach Dip

Makes about
3½ Cups Dip

1 package (10 ounces) frozen, chopped spinach, thawed and squeezed dry

2 packages (8 ounces each) lump crab meat or imitation crab meat

1 pint (2 cups) sour cream

½ cup mayonnaise

1 envelope dried vegetable soup mix

1 tablespoon Dijon mustard

1 tablespoon Sriracha sauce

1 tablespoon chopped or snipped fresh chives

1 lemon, juiced

Combine in large bowl.

Chill at least 2 hours.

Serve with assorted crudités and crackers.

TIP:
For Crudités and Cracker Suggestions, use sliced carrots, zucchini, peppers, broccoli, thinly sliced toasted Italian bread, cheese or herb flavored crackers.

Serve chilled with preferred dippers!

Perfect not only for brunch, but also a special lunch or dinner.

Broccoli and Cheddar Quiche
with Puffed Pastry Crust

All-purpose flour

1 sheet (8 ounces) frozen puffed pastry, thawed and rolled out to 10-inch round

Preheat oven to to 375°F.

Dust 9-inch pie plate with the flour and place the pastry crust overlapping edges. Trim to fit leaving ½-inch overhang.

2 cups cooked broccoli florets (or frozen florets, thawed)

1 cup (8 ounces) shredded cheddar cheese

Add to prepared crust.

1 cup heavy cream or half and half

3 eggs

¼ cup grated Parmesan cheese

Salt and pepper

Combine in large bowl.

Pour into crust.

Bake 40 minutes or until browned and firm in center.

Makes 8 Servings

TIP:
If crust browns too quickly, cover loosely with aluminum foil.

Baked French Toast
with Bananas Foster Syrup

1 large brioche type bread or challah
(about 1 pound), cut into 1-inch-thick slices
(The braided ones look the prettiest)

} Arrange in lightly buttered,
shallow, 3 to 4-quart baking dish.

1½ cups milk
12 eggs
1½ cups heavy cream
¼ cup sugar
1 teaspoon cinnamon
½ teaspoon ground nutmeg

} Whisk until thoroughly blended in medium
bowl. Pour over bread.

2 tablespoons sugar
1 teaspoon cinnamon

} Mix in small bowl. Sprinkle over bread.

2 tablespoons butter,
cut into small pieces

} Top bread.

Cover and refrigerate for at least one hour
or overnight.

Preheat oven to 350°F.
Bake for 45 minutes or until lightly browned
and mixture is set.

Meanwhile, prepare bananas foster syrup.*

Serve French toast warm with
*Bananas Foster Syrup.

*Makes about
16 Servings*

I made this recipe for the
Millennium New Year's
Eve celebration in 2000.
A good friend, Cathy, gave
this idea to me as a great
make-ahead for overnight
guests. I added my own
spin to it for a fun treat
morning or night.

TIPS:

*Can divide recipe in half easily and prepare
in 2-quart casserole as above.*

*Add walnuts, pecans or almonds for
extra crunch.*

*Bananas Foster Syrup

¼ cup butter
¼ cup brown sugar
} *Melt in large skillet until blended.*

1 cup maple syrup
} *Add slowly to butter mixture.*

4 medium bananas, sliced
} *Add and cook 2 minutes, stirring gently or until lightly browned.*

Serve warm.

These can be served at room temperature and make a beautiful presentation on any platter.

Maple Glazed Bacon Wrapped Breadsticks

Preheat oven to 375°F.

12 hard breadsticks
(any savory flavor: rosemary,
garlic, onion, Parmesan)
24 bacon strips, uncooked

Wrap each breadstick with 2 pieces
of bacon. Place on wire rack
(a baking cooling rack works great)
inserted in shallow baking pan.

½ cup maple syrup

Brush bacon with maple syrup.

Bake 20 minutes or until crisp.

TIP:
*Tuck a rosemary sprig between
bacon and breadstick for an extra
special touch.*

*Makes
12 Servings*

A scrumptious potato side dish, even for dinner. It can be baked ahead and served at room temperature.

Potato and Egg Strata *with* Fontina, Swiss and Mozzarella

Preheat oven to 400°F.

2 tablespoons butter
1 small red onion, chopped
1 red pepper, chopped

Cook over medium heat in large skillet, about 5 minutes.

1 bag (30 ounces) frozen hash browns, thawed

Add and lightly brown.
Press mixture in single layer, in lightly greased 13 x 9-inches baking dish or shallow casserole.

6 slices bacon, cooked and crumbled
2 cups shredded cheese
(combination of Fontina, Cheddar, and Swiss)

Sprinkle over hash brown mixture.

8 eggs, slightly beaten
1 cup milk
Salt and pepper

Combine in large bowl of electric mixer.
Pour into casserole.
Bake 30 minutes or until brown.

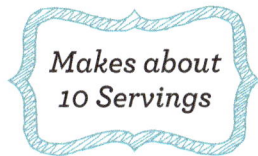

Makes about 10 Servings

Garnish, if desired, with sliced green onion or chives.

Berry-ful Lemony Scones

Preheat oven to 400°F.

2 cups all-purpose flour
¼ cup sugar
2 teaspoons baking powder
½ teaspoon salt

Combine in large bowl.

¼ cup (½ stick) chilled butter,
cut into small pieces

Stir into flour mixture gently until well-combined until mixture resembles coarse crumbs.

½ cup half and half or light cream
1 egg, slightly beaten
1 lemon, zested and juiced

Add to flour mixture until just combined.

½ cup each blueberries, raspberries
and sliced strawberries (or combination
of any berry to make 1½ cups)

*Add gently to batter mixture.
With floured hands, turn dough onto baking sheet lined with parchment paper. Shape into flat circle about ½-inch thick. Slice down with long sharp knife into 8 triangles.*

1 tablespoon half and half or light cream

Brush on dough.

1 tablespoon sugar

Sprinkle over dough.

*Makes
8 Scones*

*Bake for 20 to 25 minutes or
until lightly browned.*

A make-ahead for early and surprise guests.

Marisa's Triple Threat Berry Muffins

Preheat oven to 400°F.
Lightly grease muffin pans, or line with paper baking cups. Set aside.

2 cup all-purpose flour
1 tablespoon baking powder
1 teaspoon salt
¼ cup sugar

} *Combine in large bowl.*

2 eggs
1 cup milk
½ cup (1 stick) butter, melted
1 teaspoon vanilla extract
1 lemon, zested

} *Combine in large bowl.*
Add to flour mixture and stir
until just combined.

3 cups berries
(1 cup each blueberries, raspberries,
and/or blackberries)

} *Add to batter and gently mix.*
Spoon batter into prepared muffin pans.

1 tablespoon lemon zest

} *Sprinkle on batter.*

Bake 20 minutes or until toothpick
inserted in center comes out clean.

Makes
12 Muffins

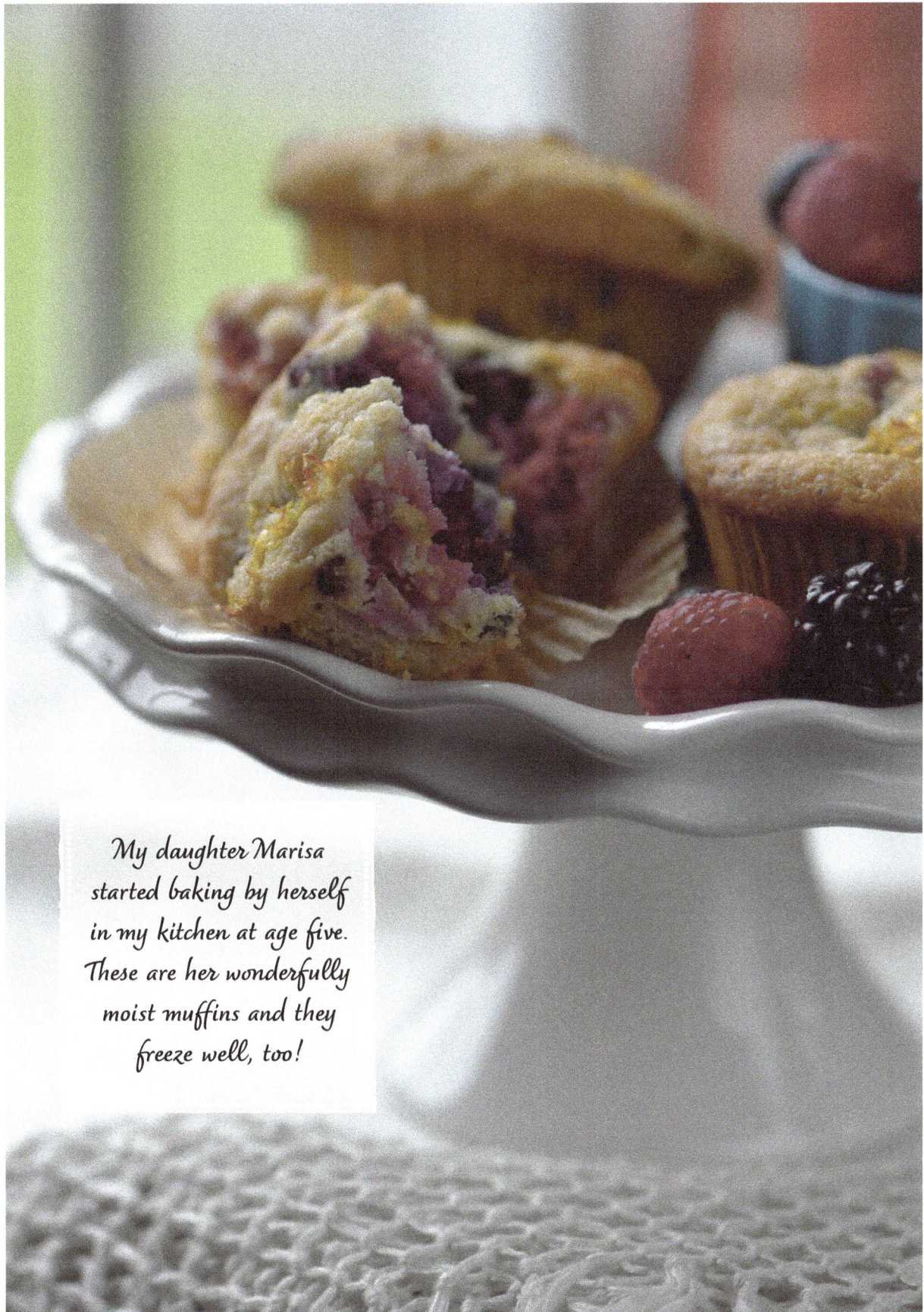

My daughter Marisa
started baking by herself
in my kitchen at age five.
These are her wonderfully
moist muffins and they
freeze well, too!

This recipe was inspired by a sweet friend, and colleague, Denise, who shared this recipe at our shoots while working on set. Tender cake underneath a mountain of huge decadent crumb topping.

Super Huge Crumb Cake

Preheat oven to 350°F.

*Line 9 x 13-inch baking pan with heavy-duty aluminum foil, extended
over edges of pan. Spray with non-stick cooking spray, line with parchment paper
and spray again. (Remember BPB: The butter, paper, butter rule in baking.)
This prevents cake from sticking to bottom of pan and create easy removal. Set aside.*

2 cups all-purpose flour*
1 teaspoon baking powder
1 teaspoon baking soda
1/2 teaspoon salt

Combine in large bowl and set aside.

1/2 cup (1 stick) butter, softened
1 cup sugar

*Add to large bowl of electric mixer and beat
until light and creamy, about 5 minutes.*

2 eggs
1 cup sour cream
2 teaspoons vanilla extract

*Add to the butter and sugar mixture and
beat on medium speed about 2 minutes or
until smooth.*

*Slowly add the flour mixture and beat for
2 minutes or until smooth.*

**Makes
16 Servings**

4 cups all-purpose flour
2/3 cup light brown sugar
2/3 cup sugar
1 teaspoon vanilla extract
1 teaspoon cinnamon

*Pour into prepared pan and bake for
20 minutes.*

Combine in large bowl while cake bakes.

3 sticks (1 1/2 cups) butter, melted

*Add to flour mixture and stir until
combined and lumpy.*

TIP:
*Substitute the cake batter using
1 box (15.25 ounces) yellow or devil's food
cake mix prepared according to package
directions with the addition of 1/2 cup
sour cream. Bake as above.*

*Top cake with crumb mixture and bake
additional 15 to 20 minutes or until
toothpick inserted in center is clean and
topping is lightly browned.*

*Sprinkle, if desired, with confectioner's
sugar. Cut into squares.*

Lemon Curd Tarts

3 large eggs

½ cup sugar

½ cup fresh lemon juice
(about 3 to 4 lemons)

Whisk in a double boiler over simmering water, stirring constantly, until thick, 5 to 10 minutes, being careful not to scramble the eggs. Remove from heat.

¼ cup butter (½ stick)

Add to egg mixture and stir until well incorporated.

1 lemon, zested

Stir into mixture.
Let cool slightly. Place plastic wrap directly on surface of lemon curd to avoid forming a skin on top. Makes about 2 cups lemon curd.

2 packages (1.9 ounces each) frozen phyllo mini tart shells, cooked according to package directions, let cool.

Spoon into prepared tart shells. Garnish, if desired, with fresh whipped cream and additional lemon zest.

*Makes about
30 Tarts*

TIPS:

The lemon curd can be made ahead and refrigerated up to one week.

Fill tart shells one hour ahead before your guests arrive to keep shells crisp.

These tarts will be a beautiful addition to your dessert buffet. The phyllo cups make preparation easy, and the lemon curd can be made ahead of time.

A coconut, chocolate
and almond lover's
dessert all in one.

Toasted Coconut, Almond and Chocolate Cake

Preheat oven to 350°F.

Spray 2 (9-inch) round cake pans lightly with non-stick cooking spray, line bottom with parchment paper and spray again. (Remember BPB: The butter, paper, butter rule in baking.) This prevents cake from sticking to bottom of pan and create easy removal. Set aside.

1 box (15.25 ounces) chocolate devil's or fudge cake mix

1 package (3.9 ounces) instant chocolate pudding

1 cup sour cream

1 cup unsweetened coconut cream*

3 eggs

2 tablespoons instant espresso coffee

1 teaspoon coconut extract

1 teaspoon vanilla extract

Makes about 16 Servings

Combine in large bowl of electric mixer. Mix on high speed 2 minutes.

Pour into prepared pans.

Bake 35 to 40 minutes or until done.

Cool on wire rack.

Frosting:

8 ounces (2 packages) cream cheese, softened

1 cup (2 sticks) butter, softened

2 boxes (1 pound each) confectioner's sugar

1 teaspoon coconut extract

1 teaspoon vanilla extract

Combine in large bowl of electric mixer.

Start on low speed until combined (or you will have powdered sugar all over you!) and then mix on high speed until smooth and fluffy.

1 cup sweetened flaked coconut

2 cups sweetened flaked coconut, toasted**

1½ cups sliced almonds, toasted

To assemble, place one cake layer on serving plate.

Top with ⅓ frosting mixture. Sprinkle with 1 cup untoasted coconut.

Top with second cake layer.

Generously spread with remaining frosting.

Sprinkle and pat toasted coconut on top and sides of cake.

Top center with toasted sliced almonds.

Chill at least 2 hours to hold together.

TIPS:

*Can substitute with unsweetened coconut milk.

**To toast coconut, spread on foil-lined baking sheet and bake in a 375°F oven for about 10 minutes. Stir several times since it will brown on the edges first.

Cake layers can be frozen up to three weeks. Cake can be frosted two days ahead and chilled in refrigerator.

Dinner *with* Friends

White Potato Pizza *with* Rosemary and Pignoli Nuts

Pizza Dough Perfetto

Baked Artichoke Dip *with* Semolina Bread Topping

Sonny's Famous Eggplant Meatballs

Skewered Antipasto Kebobs

Broccoli, Nut and Fruit Chopped Salad

Chicken Cutlets

Sweetened Ricotta Bruschetta *with* Fig Jam

Farfalle Pasta *with* Fresh Spinach Pesto

Broccoli Rabe *with* Sausage and Cannellini Beans

Baby Green Salad *with* Goat Cheese, Dried Cherries
and Cinnamon Roasted Pecans

Black and White Chocolate Chip Cookies

Cassis Drizzled Berry Fruit Compote

Flakey Pie Pastry Crust

Coconut Cream Pie

Chocolate Hazelnut Torte

White Potato Pizza *with* Rosemary and Pignoli Nuts

1 pound fresh pizza dough* (see page 42)

2 tablespoons extra virgin olive oil

1 tablespoon cornmeal

Preheat oven to 400°F.

Brush olive oil in 12½ x 17½ x 1-inch half sheet pan or 14-inch pizza pan.

Sprinkle with cornmeal. This gives the pizza a rustic brick oven look and feel.

Press pizza dough to the edges of prepared pan. Let rest uncovered 30 minutes.

Bake 8 to 10 minutes or until lightly browned. (At this point, pizza can be wrapped and frozen up to 3 weeks).

Makes about 12 Servings

¼ cup extra virgin olive oil

4 cloves of garlic, finely chopped

5 (3-inch) sprigs of rosemary, leaves removed

½ teaspoon salt

⅛ teaspoon ground pepper

Combine in 1-cup heatproof glass measuring cup. Microwave for 1 minute. Set aside. (Note: Can also heat mixture in small saucepan over low heat, 5 minutes.) This infuses the olive oil with rosemary and sweetens the garlic by removing it's raw bitter flavor.

4 to 5 medium red bliss potatoes, sliced ⅛-inch thick

Cook in boiling water for 5 minutes, or until fork tender. Drain and let cool.

¼ cup grated Pecorino Romano cheese

Brush pizza dough lightly with half of the olive oil mixture. Sprinkle with Pecorino Romano cheese.

8 ounces fresh mozzarella, sliced or shredded

Place potatoes in single layer on dough. Brush with remaining olive oil mixture. Place mozzarella evenly over potatoes.

½ cup shaved or grated Parmigiano Reggiano cheese

¼ cup pignoli nuts (pine nuts)

Top evenly.

Raise oven temperature to 425°F.

Bake for 10 minutes on top rack of oven. Move to bottom rack and bake 10 more minutes or until golden and crispy.

TIPS:

*Can also use defrosted, store-bought frozen pizza dough or purchase from local pizzeria.

Can also be baked on pizza stone for extra crispy crust.

Let it rest 5 minutes before cutting. Kitchen shears work best.

Cut them into squares or wedges. Also delicious served at room temperature.

Cut into 8 squares for an entree or 24 triangles for an appetizer.

Can assemble pizza ahead and freeze. Do not defrost frozen pizza. Bake at 425°F as above.

Your mouth will water when you begin to smell this infused olive oil with rosemary and garlic combination draped over potato pizza. You will never eat another white pizza like this.

Pizza Dough Perfetto

1 envelope (.75 ounces) dry yeast, about 2½ teaspoons

1 cup warm water*

} Combine in glass measuring cup or medium bowl. (NOTE: After a few minutes the mixture should become foamy. This is proof that the yeast is active and alive for proper rising.)

2½ cups unbleached all-purpose flour**, divided

} Add 2 cups flour onto lightly floured wooden board. Make a well in center to form a circle using a custard cup.

Add remaining flour to center.

1 tablespoon extra virgin olive oil

2 teaspoons salt

} Add olive oil and salt to the center. Slowly add yeast mixture to the center stirring with a fork. Continue mixing with the fork from the outside circle to the center until mixture starts to come together. (NOTE: At this point I start to use a bench scraper to bring it all together. Mixture will be loose and slightly wet.)

Makes enough dough for a 12½ x 17½ x 1-inch pan (½ sheet pan or 14-inch pizza pan) or 1 stromboli

Start to knead, add a little sprinkle of flour if dough is too sticky, for about 5 minutes. Add additional sprinkling of flour, a little at a time if needed. (My Nana would say "Knead until the dough feels as smooth as a baby's bottom.") Form into a ball. When you press the center of the dough with your finger and it springs back, it's done!

1 tablespoon extra virgin olive oil

} Brush on bowl. Add dough, turn to coat. Cover with damp cloth or with plastic wrap.

Keep at room temperature or a little warmer for 1 to 2 hours, until dough doubles in size. Continue according to Pizza recipes (pages 40 and 152) and Stromboli recipe (page 152).

TIPS:
*Water temperature should be between 105-115°F.
Be careful water isn't too hot or it will kill the yeast and dough won't rise!
**Can substitute with one cup 00 flour or bread flour for a more dense and chewy crust.
Can store in refrigerator covered, for one day until ready to use.
Bring to room temperature before using.
Dough can be prepared and frozen for up to two months ahead.
Allow to thaw at room temperature before using.

Homemade pizza making made easy! I always use this recipe when family visits from Colorado. My big sister, Celeste, says "Alyssa's pizza is the first thing I crave when I come to New Jersey, and it always starts with her flawless dough."

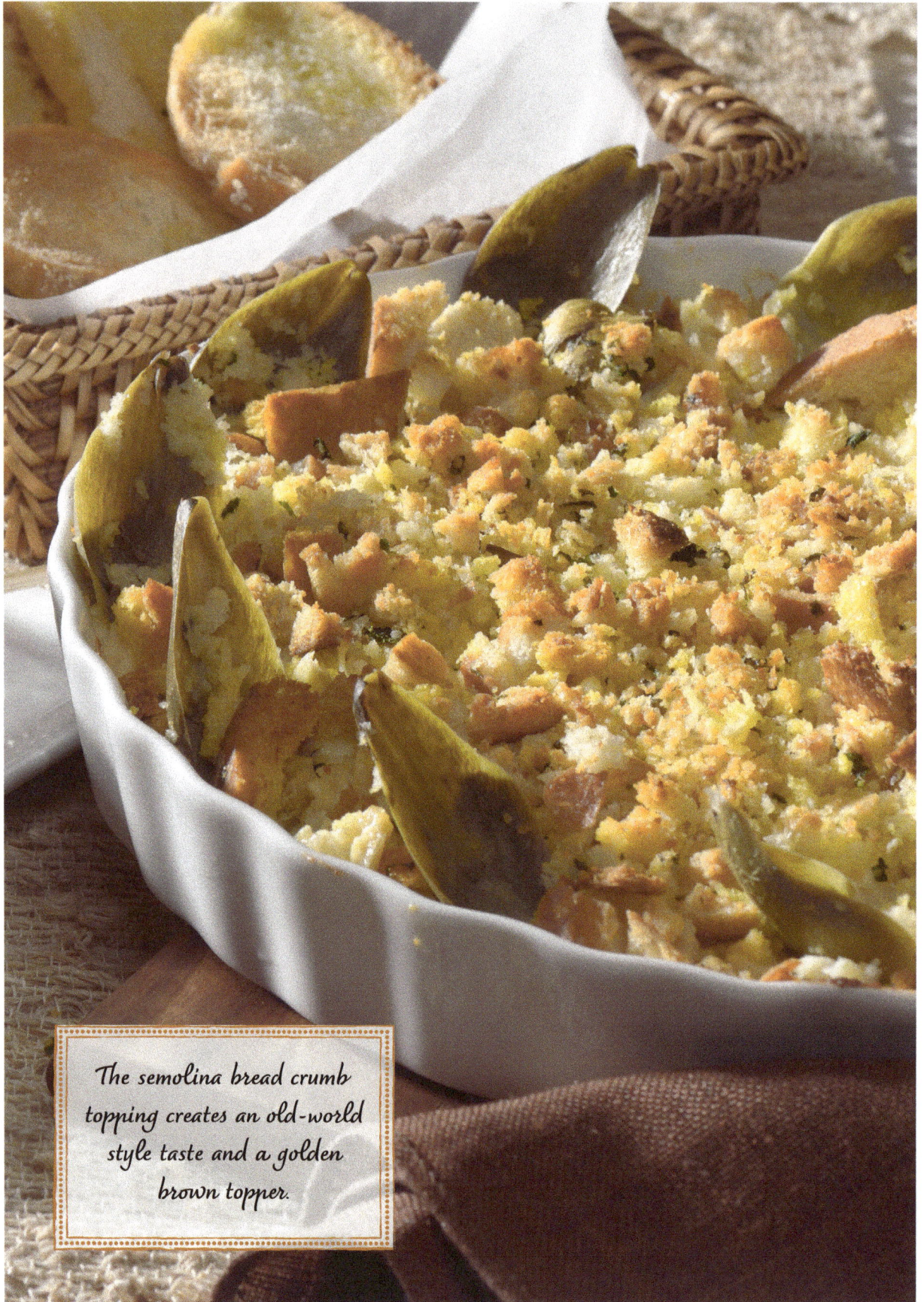

The semolina bread crumb topping creates an old-world style taste and a golden brown topper.

Baked Artichoke Dip *with* Semolina Bread Topping

1 cup fresh breadcrumbs
(Italian or Semolina bread, processed in
food processer until fine)*
2 tablespoons grated Parmesan cheese
2 tablespoons grated Pecorino Romano cheese
3 tablespoons extra virgin olive oil
1 clove garlic, chopped
1 tablespoon chopped Italian parsley

Preheat oven to 350°F.

Combine in small bowl and set aside.

½ cup grated Parmesan cheese
½ cup grated Pecorino Romano cheese
1 clove garlic, chopped
1 can (14 ounces) artichoke hearts in water,
drained
1 jar (12 ounces) marinated artichoke
hearts, drained
¾ cup mayonnaise
½ cup sour cream or Greek plain yogurt
Salt and pepper

Combine in food processor.

Process with just pulses until
almost blended but still chunky.

Turn into lightly greased 9-inch baking
dish/quiche pan or 1-pint casserole dish.

Top with bread crumb mixture.

Bake for 20 minutes or until heated through.

*Variation: For lighter version use low fat
mayonnaise and/or reduced fat sour cream.*

TIPS:

**Can substitute with Panko or plain dried
breadcrumbs.*

*Serve with grilled or toasted, sliced Italian
bread rubbed with garlic and drizzled with
extra virgin olive oil, sprinkled with your
favorite herbs.*

*Surround with fresh artichoke leaves,
blanched.*

*Entire recipe can be made one day ahead
and chilled until ready to bake.*

*Makes about
16 Servings*

Sonny's Famous Eggplant Meatballs

¼ cup extra virgin olive oil

6 cloves garlic, chopped

1 Vidalia onion, chopped (about 1½ cups)

} *Cook on medium heat in large deep skillet until translucent and soft, about 10 minutes.*

2 medium eggplants or one large, peeled and cut into small cubes (about 12 cups)

1 cup water

} *Add to skillet and cook over low heat, about 30 to 50 minutes (depends on eggplant) or until very very soft (like mush). OR bake the eggplants whole with skin on, 30 minutes or until fork tender. Peel and chop and add to skillet. Omit water.*

½ cup dry white wine

} *Add to skillet and let cook over medium heat, 10 more minutes. Let cool.*

½ loaf Italian bread (about ½ pound) torn into small pieces, about 4 cups

1 to 1½ cups water

} *Mix in large bowl and let soak 15 minutes or until soft.*

1 cup (4 ounces) fresh mozzarella, shredded

½ cup grated Parmesan cheese

½ cup grated Pecorino Romano cheese

8 ounces (about 2½ cups) grated ricotta salata

1 cup panko bread crumbs*

1 egg

1 bunch flat leaf Italian parsley, chopped (about 1 cup)

¼ chopped fresh basil

} *Add to bread mixture.*

½ lemon, juiced

Salt and pepper

} *Add to eggplant mixture.*

Mix well; chill for at least 30 minutes.

Add eggplant mixture to bread crumb mixture.

Stir to combine.

*Note: If mixture holds together when squeezed it's ready to roll. If very wet add little more panko crumbs until mixture holds together.

Scoop with 2-inch ice cream scoop, or ¼ cup measuring cup and roll into balls.

Makes about 14 Servings, 42 Meatballs

1½ cups panko crumbs

1 tablespoon each grated Parmesan and Pecorino Romano Cheese

}

Place in shallow plate and roll balls into bread crumbs.

Either fry in large skillet with canola oil ¼-inch deep with one swirl olive oil until browned, about 3 to 5 minutes, OR place on well greased baking sheets (drizzle with a little additional extra virgin olive oil) and bake at 375°F for 25 minutes or until golden.

Serve with my Fresh Marinara Sauce recipe (See page 167) over meatballs with extra grated ricotta salata and grated Parmesan. Great over your favorite pasta!

See page 167

TIPS:

Can be frozen up to two months.

Use a 1½-inch ice cream scoop or heaping tablespoon and make mini eggplant meatballs for a fun appetizer. Makes about 75 mini meatballs.

When my family had our restaurant, Sonny's on the Avenue, our customers' favorite item was our Eggplant Meatballs which do not have any meat in them. They were inspired by my husband's friend Paulie. They were featured as an appetizer but also served as an entree over pasta. They will be a hit with your family as much as they are with ours!

Skewered Antipasto Kebobs

2 tablespoons white balsamic vinegar

¼ cup extra virgin olive oil

1 lemon, zested and juiced

¼ cup fresh basil, thinly sliced and chopped

Salt and pepper

} *Combine in small bowl. Set aside.*

8 (8-inch) wooden skewers

16 mini fresh mozzarella balls
(often labeled ciliegine)

16 red and/or yellow cherry tomatoes

16 slices (½ inch thick) pepperoni

16 fresh basil leaves

} *Skewer alternately.*

Brush with vinaigrette before serving.

Serve with extra basil vinaigrette.

*Makes
8 Servings*

TIPS:
Can be made a few hours ahead.
Can substitute with grape tomatoes, too!

A simple antipasto
all on one skewer!

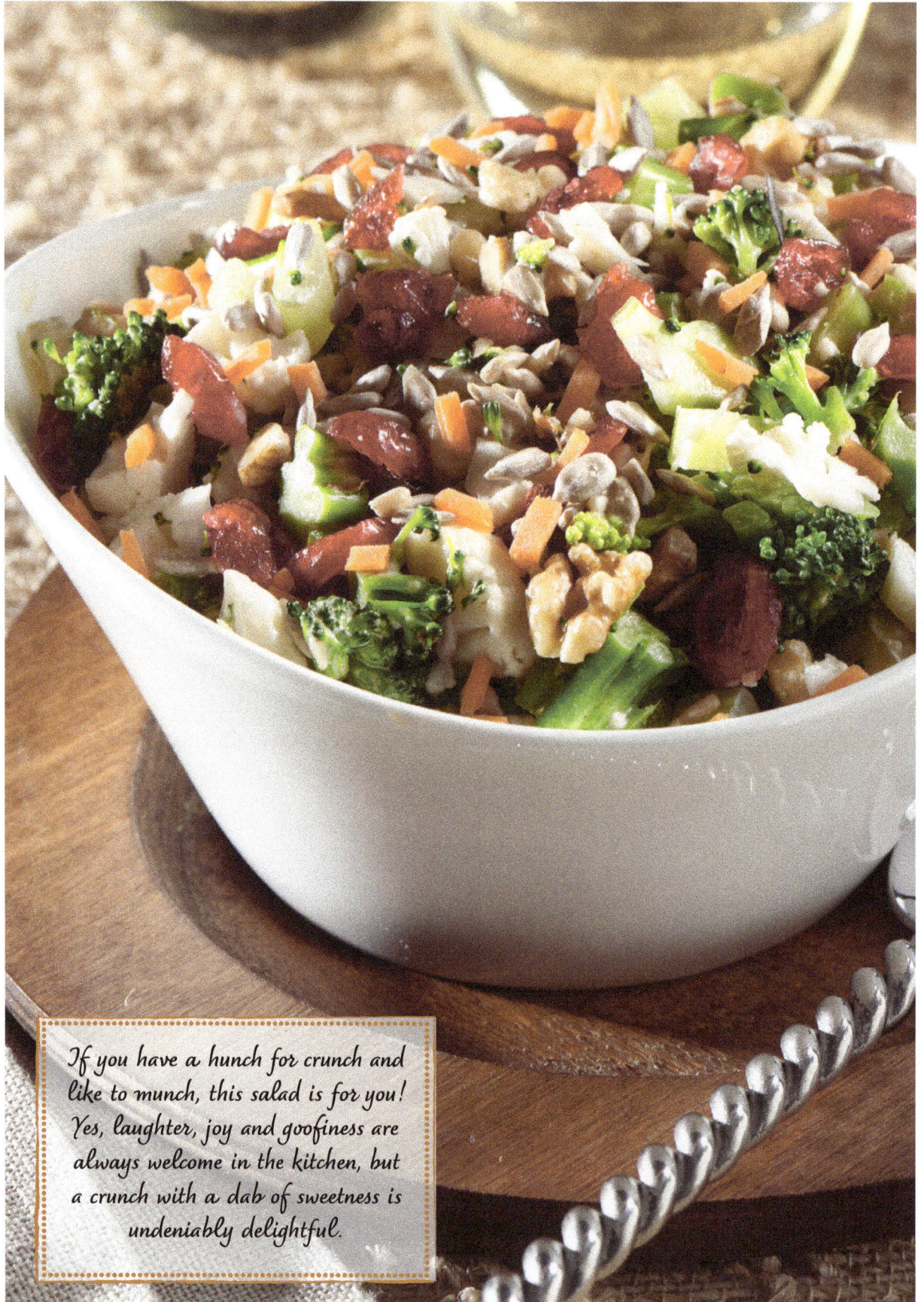

If you have a hunch for crunch and like to munch, this salad is for you! Yes, laughter, joy and goofiness are always welcome in the kitchen, but a crunch with a dab of sweetness is undeniably delightful.

Broccoli, Nut and Fruit Chopped Salad

¾ cup mayonnaise

⅓ cup raspberry vinegar

¼ cup extra virgin olive oil

2 tablespoons Dijon mustard

Salt and pepper

Combine in small bowl.

1 medium head broccoli, finely chopped (include stems, about 6 cups)

1 head cauliflower, finely chopped (include stems, about 6 cups)

2 cups shredded carrots

6 celery stalks, chopped, about 2 cups

2 cups raisins

2 cups dried cherries or cranberries

1 cup sunflower seeds

2 cups chopped walnuts

Combine in large bowl.

Toss with mayonnaise mixture to coat.

Serve immediately or chill until ready to serve.

Makes about 20 Servings

TIPS:

Chop all vegetables one day ahead, then toss with dressing the day of serving.

Recipe can be easily halved.

My youngest daughter Marisa would say, "Smelling the chicken cutlets while doing homework upstairs made me rush down to the kitchen. I couldn't wait until the first batch was done, as I'd steal a cutlet, and share a piece with our toy poodle, Lili, somehow always becoming full before dinner since they're that irresistible,"

Chicken Cutlets

1 cup all-purpose flour

½ teaspoon salt

¼ teaspoon ground pepper

} *Combine on first plate.*

4 large eggs, beaten

½ cup grated Parmesan cheese

2 lemons, juiced

1 tablespoon extra virgin olive oil

} *Combine on second plate.*

2 cups fresh breadcrumbs
(Italian or Semolina bread, processed in
food processer until fine)*

1 cup panko bread crumbs

1 bunch Italian parsley, coarsely chopped

½ cup grated Pecorino Romano cheese

½ cup grated Parmesan cheese

} *Combine on third plate.*

2 pounds boneless chicken breasts,
thinly sliced or pounded thin

} *Dip chicken in flour, egg mixture and then bread crumb mixture to completely coat.*

Frying method:

Oil for frying (canola with a splash of extra virgin olive oil preferred), enough to fill skillet ¼-inch deep.

Heat oils on medium high heat in large deep skillet. The oil is ready if it bubbles when you drop a little egg batter into it.

Place coated chicken gently in heated skillet.

Cook 3 to 5 minutes on each side until lightly browned.

Place on paper towel lined baking sheet to cool.

Baking method:

Lightly drizzle baking sheet with olive oil and brush to coat.

Place coated chicken breasts on baking sheet.

Drizzle with additional olive oil to lightly coat.

Bake at 400° F for 15 to 20 minutes or until golden brown and crisp.

TIPS:

*Can substitute with panko or plain dried bread crumbs.

These chicken cutlets freeze beautifully! Great for sandwiches or a quick dinner.

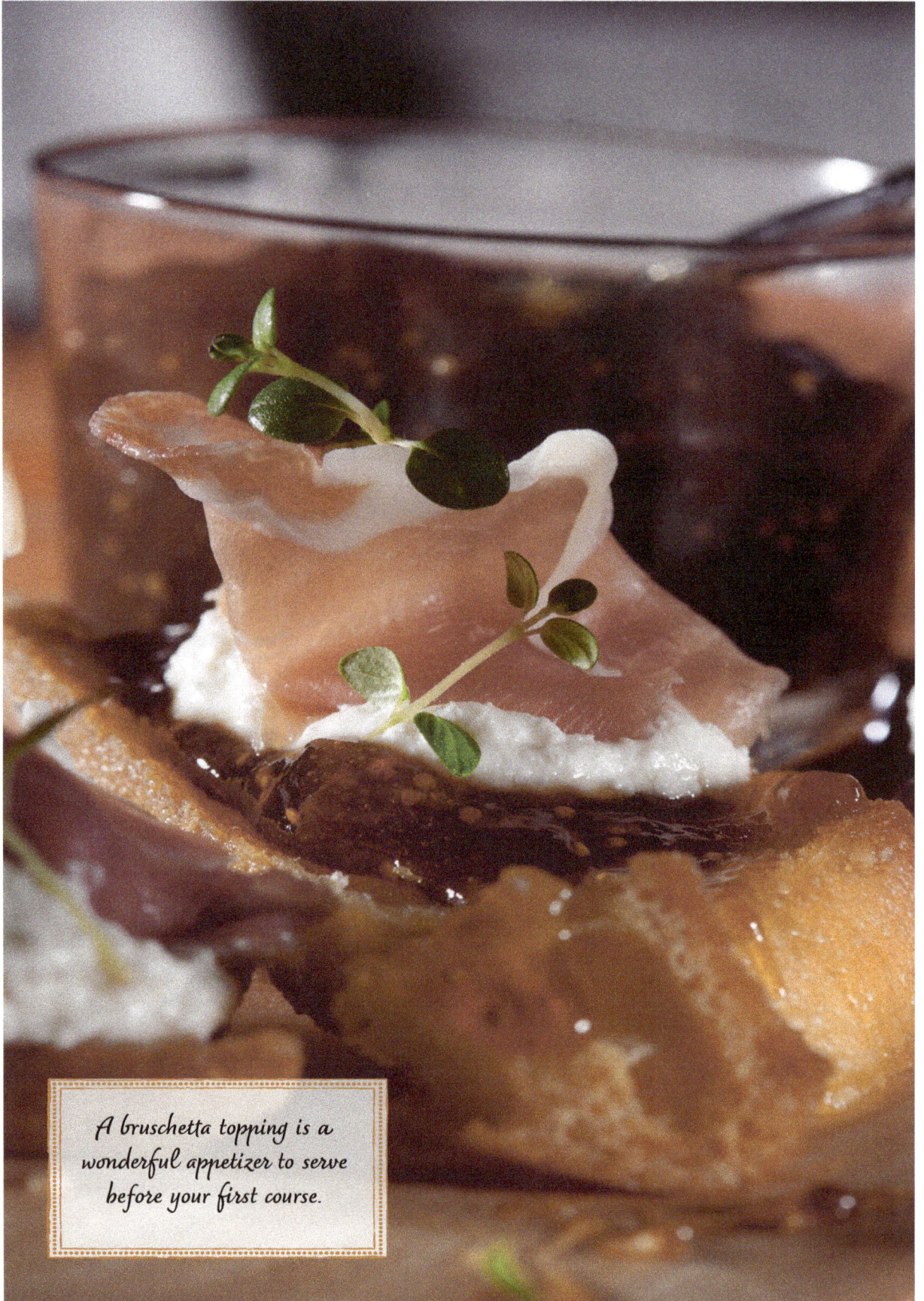

A bruschetta topping is a
wonderful appetizer to serve
before your first course.

Sweetened Ricotta Bruschetta *with* Fig Jam

1 long Italian bread, sliced thin

2 tablespoons extra virgin olive oil

¼ cup fig jam*

Preheat oven to broil.

Brush with extra virgin olive oil and then jam.

Broil until golden, about 1 to 2 minutes.

1 container (15 ounces) whole milk ricotta

2 tablespoons fig jam

Combine in small bowl and top toasted bruschetta.

6 slices prosciutto, (about 2 ounces) cut lengthwise in quarters

Fold and place on ricotta-topped bruschetta.

Top, if desired, with herbs or sprouts.

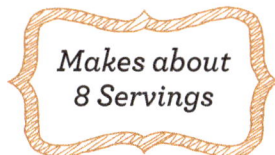

Makes about 8 Servings

TIP:
*Can substitute with raspberry or apricot preserves.

Farfalle Pasta *with* Fresh Spinach Pesto

4 cloves garlic, peeled
2 cups fresh basil leaves
1 cup Italian parsley leaves
1 cup spinach leaves

Process in food processor until smooth.

1 cup extra virgin olive oil

Drizzle in slowly while processing until blended.

½ cup grated Parmesan cheese
½ cup grated Pecorino Romano cheese
½ cup pignoli nuts (pine nuts)
Salt and pepper

Add and process until smooth.

2 boxes (1 pound each)
farfalle (bow tie pasta), cooked

Toss with pesto mixture in large bowl.

Garnish, if desired, with Parmesan cheese shavings, roasted pepper strips and additional toasted pignoli nuts.

TIPS:

Pesto can be made one week ahead of time or frozen up to one month.

Garnish with fresh basil leaves and shavings of Parmesan and Pecorino Romano cheese.

This recipe can be halved.

Makes about 8-10 Servings

This flavor is a little subtler than the traditional pesto's because the spinach keeps it extra green and gives the pasta a tang. This farfalle dish is a beautiful presentation piece and encompasses the beauty of what farfalle means in Italian, butterflies.

A staple on any Italian table, but by adding the cannellini beans, it becomes a palate pleaser for even the bitter eccentrics.

Broccoli Rabe *with* Sausage and Cannellini Beans

2 bunches broccoli rabe,
large stems removed, cut in thirds

2 teaspoons salt

Bring water to a boil in large pot.
Add and boil 3 minutes or until almost tender.

Remove using tongs or strainer and place in bowl with ice and water to stop cooking process or "shock" the veggies from overcooking.

After cooled, drain and set aside. (This can be made one day ahead; keep chilled.)

Makes about 12 Servings

3 tablespoons extra virgin olive oil

6 cloves garlic, finely chopped

1 pinch crushed red pepper flakes

Heat oil in large skillet, 1 minute.
Add garlic with hot red pepper flakes and cook over medium high heat until lightly golden. Add broccoli rabe and toss to coat. Place in large bowl.

3 pounds sweet Italian sausage links

Add to same skillet and cook on medium high heat until browned, about 5 minutes (can do this in batches). Slice on diagonal into 1-inch pieces and brown again. (Can also brown in oven on 350°F for 20 minutes or until done and slice as above.)

¼ cup white wine

Add to same large skillet and let boil off, about 1 minute.

2 cans (15.5 ounces to 16 ounces each) cannellini beans, drained

Salt and pepper

Add with prepared broccoli rabe and toss all ingredients together. Add mixture to skillet with sausage. Heat through. Serve, if desired, with grated Parmesan cheese.

TIPS:

This recipe can be easily halved.

*Can blanch broccoli rabe one day ahead, and assemble the day of the dinner.
Blanching the broccoli rabe removes the bitterness and also keeps its bright green color.*

*Can also combine all cooked ingredients at the end, in large baking or roasting pan.
Reheat in oven before serving. Drizzle with a little extra chicken broth
if mixture needs extra moisture.*

Baby Green Salad *with* Goat Cheese, Dried Cherries and Cinnamon Roasted Pecans

Preheat oven to 350°F.

1 bag (16 ounces) pecan halves, about 2 cups

} *Spread in single layer in foil-lined baking sheet sprayed with non-stick cooking spray.*

1 egg white

¼ cup sugar

2 teaspoons cinnamon

} *Mix and pour over nuts and toss well.*

2 tablespoons butter, cut into small pieces

} *Dot on nut mixture. Bake 15 minutes or until dry and crisp, stirring occasionally (do not burn). Set aside and cool. Can store for 1 week in air-tight container.*

1 container (16 ounces) field greens or mixed greens

1 head radicchio, sliced

3 bulbs Belgian endives, sliced thin lengthwise

} *Toss in large bowl or serving platter.*

1 bag (5 ounces) dried cherries (can substitute cranberries)

1 package (8 or 10 ounces) goat cheese, sliced ¼-inch and then quartered

¼ cup raspberries

} *Top with cherries, goat cheese and pecans. Top with raspberries for garnish, if desired. Serve with Raspberry Vinaigrette.*

Raspberry Vinaigrette

Makes about 8-10 Servings

1 tablespoon grainy Dijon mustard

⅓ cup raspberry vinegar

1 tablespoon honey

1 tablespoon sugar

1 lemon, zested and juiced

} *Whisk together.*

¾ cup extra virgin olive oil

} *Continue to whisk and slowly drizzle into vinegar mixture until well combined.*

1 tablespoon fresh snipped chives

1 cup raspberries, slightly crushed

Salt and pepper

} *Stir in and set aside until ready to use. Dressing can be made one day ahead.*

A salad with a sweet and salty kick — everything you wished a green salad could be.

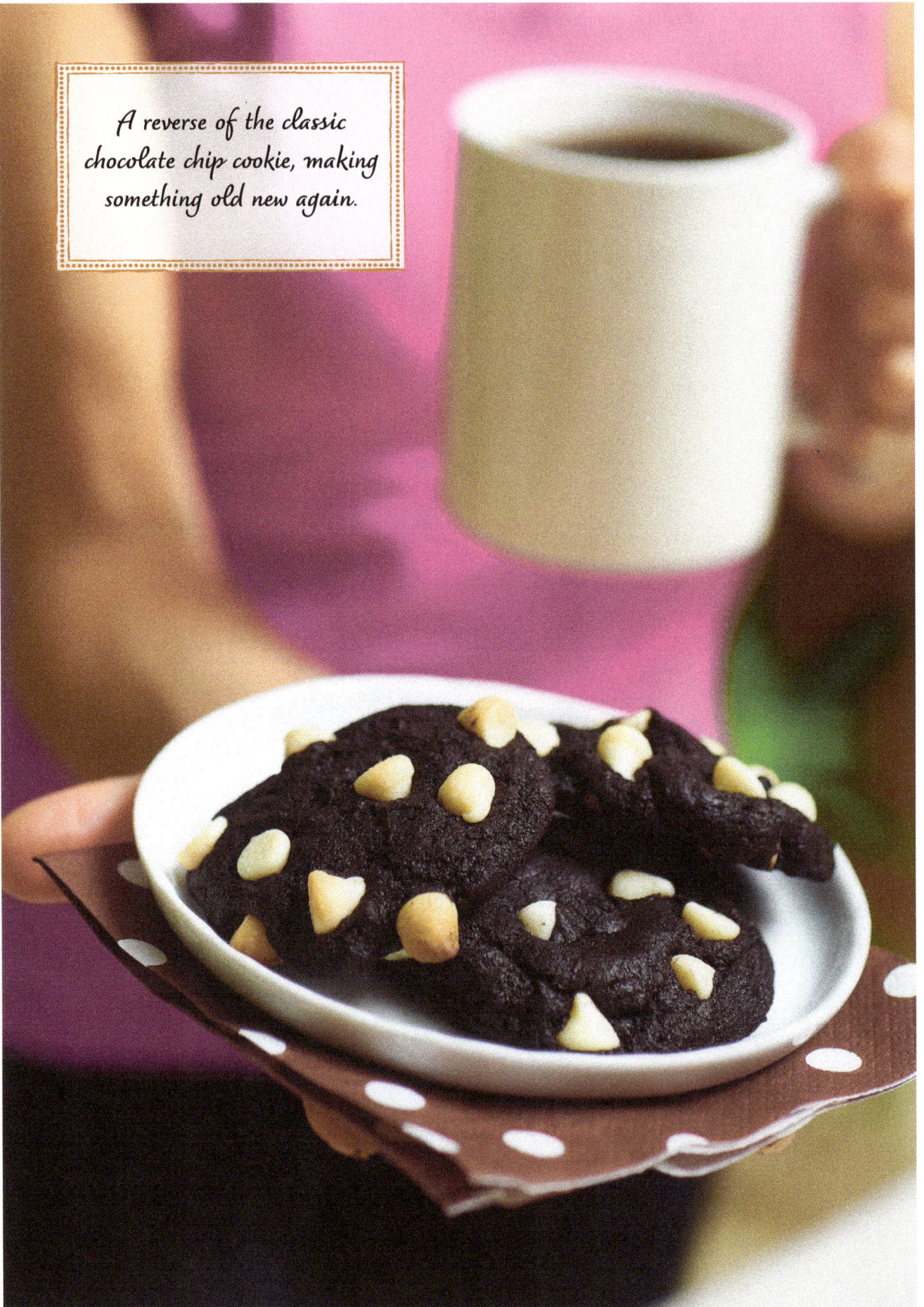

Black and White Chocolate Chip Cookies

2 cups all-purpose flour
½ cup unsweetened cocoa powder
1 teaspoon salt
1 teaspoon baking soda

Preheat oven to 350°F.

Combine in large bowl and set aside.

1 cup (2 sticks) butter, softened
1 cup granulated sugar

In large bowl of electric mixer, beat on medium high speed until creamy and light.

2 large eggs, beaten
1 tablespoon vanilla extract

Add into butter mixture until blended.
Slowly add flour mixture.

2 cups white chocolate chips

Stir in and mix until blended.

Drop rounded tablespoons about 2-inches apart on greased or parchment lined cookie sheet.

Bake 8 to 10 minutes or until set and done.

Makes 24 Cookies

TIPS:

*Can add your favorite nuts, too.
Just add 1 cup to the batter.*

Can bake and freeze one month ahead.

Cassis Drizzled Berry Fruit Compote

4 cups mixed berries: raspberries, blueberries, blackberries

} *Add to bowl.*

¼ cup créme de cassis liqueur (black currant liqueur)

1 orange, zested

2 tablespoons sugar

} *Combine and toss with berries.*
Serve, if desired, with fresh mint.

Makes 8 Servings

TIPS:

Perfect for summer as well.
Serve with your favorite sorbet or ice cream.

Ever so berry beautiful!

Flaky and flavorful!

Flakey Pie Pastry Dough for Single Crust

1¾ cups all-purpose flour

½ teaspoon salt

Combine in food processor and pulse two to three times.

¾ cup (1½ sticks) chilled unsalted butter, cut up into ½-inch cubes

Add to food processor and pulse until flour looks like small peas. (DO NOT OVER PROCESS. This will cause butter to melt and make dough tough).

4 to 5 tablespoons Ice Water or more, if needed

(Ice Water: Place a few ice cubes in ½ cup of water)

Slowly add and pulse several times until dough JUST comes together when squeezed. If the dough falls apart, and 2 to 4 more tablespoons of ice water and pulse a couple of times until it JUST starts to form a ball. Wrap in plastic wrap. Chill, 15 minutes. Let sit at room temperature 5 to 10 minutes before rolling.

Lightly flour surface, top of dough and rolling pin. Roll dough gently to 10-inch circle, about ⅛-inch thick.

Lightly dust 9 to 10-inch pie plate with flour. Gently place rolled pastry onto floured pie plate.

Press into pie plate. Flute edge by pinching pastry dough between thumb and forefinger to crimp.

Makes 1 Single Crust

*Brush with Egg Wash. Freeze prepared pie plate 10 minutes before baking, to prevent the crimped edges from shrinking during baking.

NOTE: Use directions above for recipes calling for UNBAKED pie pastry.

NOTE: Use directions below for recipes calling for BAKED pie pastry.

Preheat oven to 425°F.

Poke the sides and bottom of the pastry dough with tines of fork 12 times.

Brush pastry dough with Egg Wash.*

Bake, 10 to 15 minutes or until golden.

Let cool before filling.

TIPS:

*EGG WASH: Mix 1 egg yolk with 1 teaspoon water. Brush on pastry dough before baking for golden glow.

Pastry dough can be made two days ahead and kept wrapped in refrigerator. Also, freezes beautifully up to one month.

Can freeze dough whole, wrapped in plastic wrap. Or, press it into pie plate, wrap in plastic wrap, and freeze up to one month. Then, it's ready to be filled and baked easily!

This recipe was inspired by the Claremont Diner in West Orange, New Jersey.
It was a classic place to stop by after a night of dancing at the Meadowbrook in Cedar Grove
in the late 1940's and early 1950's. My parents fondly remembered going there and told me stories
of its delicious desserts. Here is my version of a Big Band Era favorite.
The pie is a little work, but you will think it's worth the effort after you take your first bite.

Coconut Cream Pie

Makes about 10 Servings

Preheat oven to 350°F.

2 cups flaked coconut

Baked pie pastry for single crust (see page 67)

Bake 1 cup flaked coconut on foil-lined baking sheet, 5 to 7 minutes, stirring occasionally or until lightly toasted. Set aside and reserve.

Sprinkle remaining 1 cup untoasted, flaked coconut on bottom of baked pie crust.

¼ cup cold water

1 envelope unflavored gelatin

Fill 2-cup heatproof glass measuring cup with water. Sprinkle gelatin on top. Let sit for 2 minutes to soften. Microwave on high for 30 seconds or until dissolved. Set aside and let cool.

3 large eggs

Whisk in medium saucepan until light in color.

½ cup sugar

Whisk into eggs gradually until well blended.

1 cup milk

Add to another medium saucepan and cook over low heat.
Add ¼ cup of hot milk gradually into egg mixture to temper eggs (so they don't scramble), then gradually whisk in remaining milk.

1 vanilla bean or 1 teaspoon vanilla extract

Add vanilla bean.
Cook over low heat, stirring constantly, until mixture resembles heavy cream. (DO NOT BOIL or you will have scrambled eggs.)
Pour into medium bowl and add gelatin mixture.
Chill until thickened, about 30 to 45 minutes.
Remove vanilla bean and, with paring knife, slice almost cutting through bean. Scrape vanilla seeds into chilled mixture. Discard vanilla pod.

1½ cups heavy cream

¼ cup confectioner's sugar

In large chilled stainless steel bowl of electric mixer, whip heavy cream on medium high speed, until soft peaks form.
Add confectioner's sugar gradually until blended but do not overbeat.
Stir in half of whipped cream mixture into chilled custard mixture.
Pour into prepared crust. Top or pipe remaining whipped cream to garnish top of pie.

Reserved 1 cup toasted coconut

Sprinkle on pie.

Chill at least three hours before serving.

Chocolate Hazelnut Torte

Preheat oven to 325°F.

Spray 9-inch cake pan with non-stick cooking spray or butter, line with parchment paper and spray again. (Remember BPB: The butter, paper, butter rule in baking.)
This prevents torte from sticking to bottom of pan and create easy removal. Set aside.

Batter:

1 cup hazelnuts, toasted, skins removed *

4 ounces semi-sweet or bittersweet chocolate, chopped

} *Add to food processor and blend until smooth.*

1 cup (2 sticks) butter, softened

1 cup sugar

} *Add to food processor and pulse until thoroughly blended.*

5 eggs

} *Add one at a time.*

½ cup cake flour

} *Scrape down bowl and pulse once or twice to incorporate flour.*

Fill prepared cake pan. Bake 20 to 25 minutes until cake tester comes out clean.

Wait 5 minutes, then invert on cooling rack.

Makes about 10 Servings

Ganache Topping:

1 cup heavy cream

} *Heat to just a boil in small saucepan.*

8 ounces semi-sweet or bittersweet chocolate, chopped

} *Remove saucepan from heat. Stir in until smooth.*

On wire rack, pour over cooled cake. Let set and then transfer to serving platter.

Garnish with additional whole hazelnuts and chocolate curls.

Serve, if desired, with fresh whipped cream or ice cream.

TIP:
*To remove skins from hazelnuts, bake for 10 minutes at 350°F. Place on a kitchen towel and rub off skins.

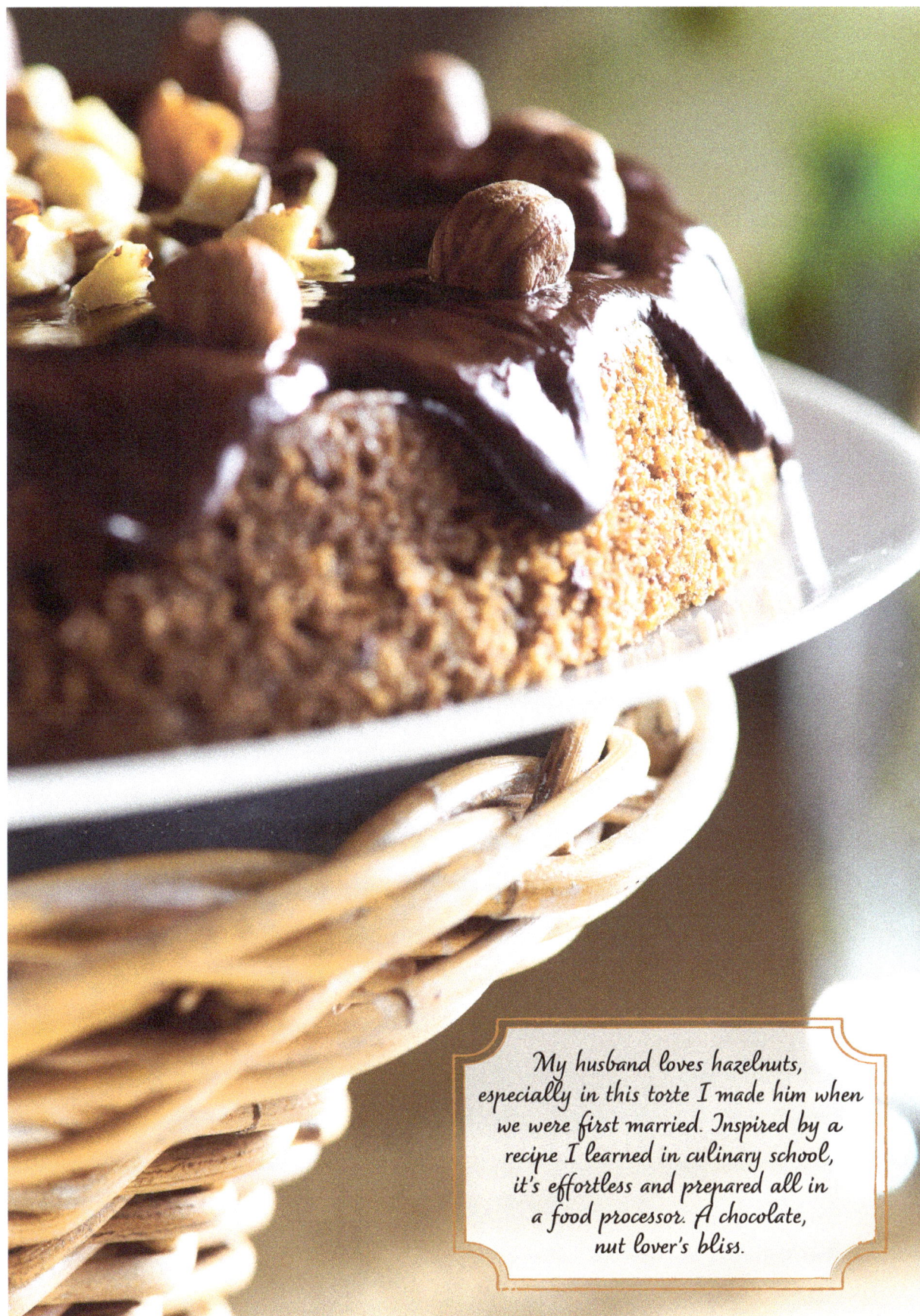

My husband loves hazelnuts, especially in this torte I made him when we were first married. Inspired by a recipe I learned in culinary school, it's effortless and prepared all in a food processor. A chocolate, nut lover's bliss.

birthday

Birthday Bash

Grilled Quesadillas

Fresh Chunky Salsa

Zesty Guacamole

Sweet 'n' Sour Chicken Wings

BBQ Cajun Style Ribs

Maple Cured Baked Beans

Barley, Corn and Edamame Salad

Grandma's Potato Salad

Sweet Onion Hot Dog Topping

Tri-Color Cole Slaw

Triple Crown Chocolate Brownies

Chocolate Covered Strawberries

Triple Layer Cannoli Cake

Grilled Quesadillas

2 cups (8 ounces) shredded Cheddar cheese
6 (10-inch) flour tortillas

} *Sprinkle evenly over half of each tortilla.*

1 medium tomato, chopped
½ cup chopped green onions or scallions
1 bunch cilantro, chopped

} *Sprinkle over cheese.**

Fold tortillas over filling.

Cook filled tortillas in heavy skillet, grill pan or grill over medium heat, 2 to 3 minutes, on each side or until golden brown and crisp.

Cut each into 3 wedges.

Serve, if desired, with sour cream, Greek yogurt, guacamole and salsa for dipping.

*Suggested Fillings:

- *Chopped chorizo, shredded Manchego cheese, hot pepper jelly*

- *Thinly sliced pears, Gorgonzola cheese, fig jam*

- *Sliced Parmesan cheese, drizzle of honey, sprinkle of rosemary*

- *Sliced tomato, sliced or shredded mozzarella, basil leaves*

*Makes
6 Servings or
18 Appetizers*

TIPS:

Substitute any type of tortilla: whole wheat, whole grain, etc.

Can be made 2 to 5 hours ahead of time on baking sheets. Cover with plastic wrap and chill until ready to grill.

Pick your
favorite filling!

Fresh Chunky Salsa

2 ripe tomatoes, chopped

1 green, yellow or orange pepper, chopped
(or combination of all three)

1 onion, chopped

1 can corn (15.25 ounces), drained

1 can black beans (15.5 ounces),
rinsed and drained

1 clove garlic, chopped

2 limes, zested and juiced

1 bunch cilantro, chopped (about 1 cup)

1 jalapeño, chopped

2 tablespoons extra virgin olive oil

Salt and pepper

In a serving bowl, combine all ingredients.

*Serve immediately or chill until ready to use.
Bring to room temperature before serving to
infuse flavors.*

Easy Peasy!

TIP:

*Add 1 cup grilled, fresh, canned or frozen
corn kernels for added color and crunch.*

Zesty Guacamole

*Makes 2 Cups
(8 Servings)*

2 cloves garlic, finely chopped

1 lime, zested and juiced

1 teaspoon salt

¼ teaspoon pepper

} *Combine in medium bowl.*

4 ripe avocados, peeled

} *Add.*
Mash with fork but still keep chunky.

1 bunch cilantro, chopped (about 1 cup)

} *Add and combine.*

TIPS:

Add 1 jalapeño, seeded and finely chopped for added spice.

Best to serve immediately but to delay browning for a little while, add back the pit and squeeze extra lime juice on top. Cover with plastic wrap.

Make this right before guests arrive and be prepared to make more!

Sweet 'n' Sour Chicken Wings

Preheat oven to 450°F.

Line 15 x 10½-inch baking pan with heavy-duty aluminum foil and spray with non-stick cooking spray.

1 jar (18 ounces) apricot marmalade*

½ cup Dijon mustard

1 bunch green onions (scallions), chopped with green tops

} *Combine in medium bowl and set aside.*

2 packages (about 1½ pounds each) chicken wingettes**

} *Spread out on prepared pan.*

Bake 20 minutes.

Add sauce mixture and stir to coat.

Bake an additional 20 minutes, turning occasionally, or until browned and crispy. For extra crispy, broil and additional 3 to 5 minutes.

Garnish, if desired, with additional green onion slices.

Makes about 8 Servings

TIPS:

* You can use any favorite marmalade to make your flavored chicken wings. Raspberry, orange and strawberry work well as substitutes.

**You can use regular chicken wings, cut in half. Remove wing tips.

Four ingredient wings that take only five minutes to put together create an instant "Ahhh" moment among guests.

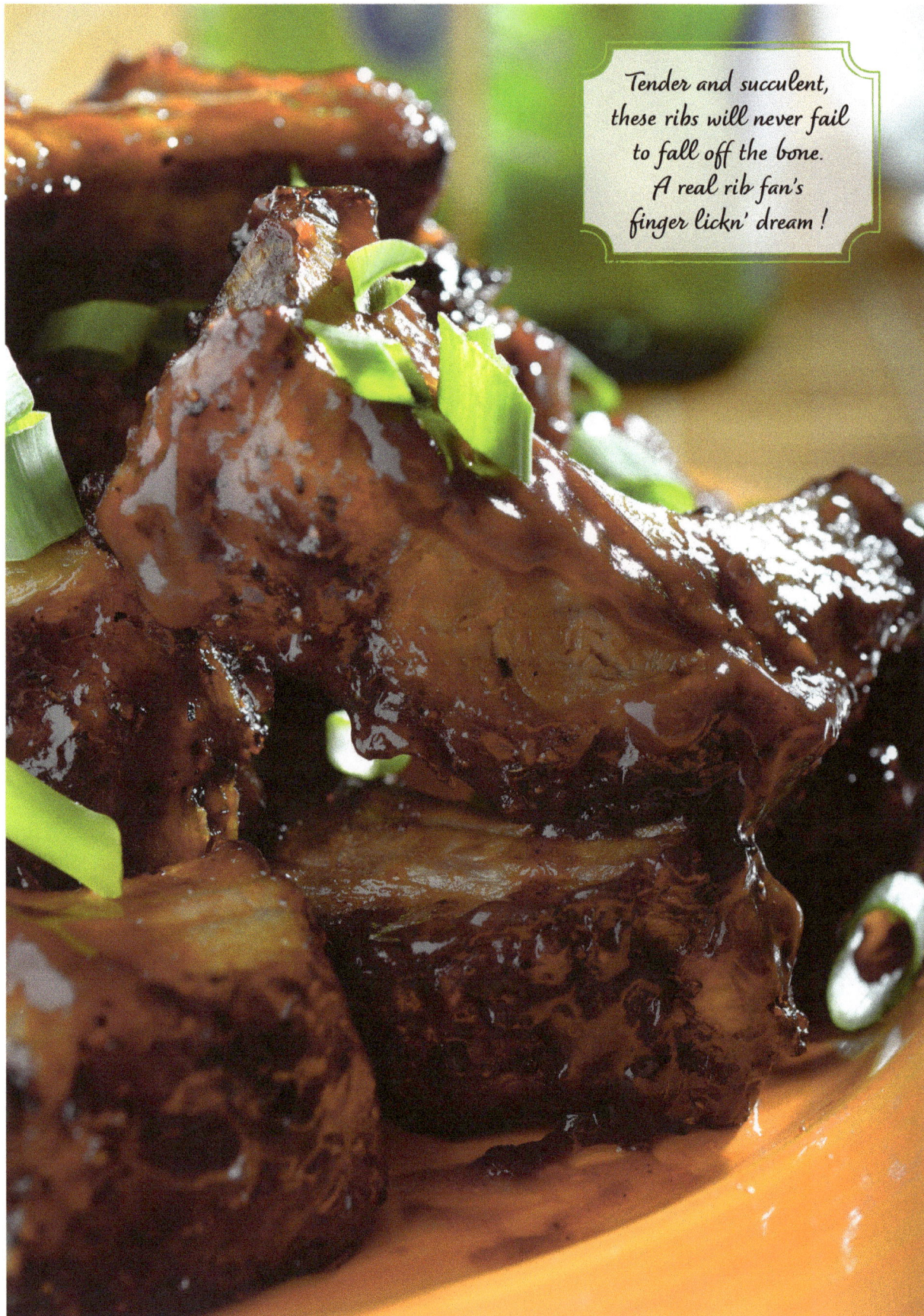

Tender and succulent, these ribs will never fail to fall off the bone. A real rib fan's finger lickn' dream!

BBQ Cajun Style Ribs

Preheat oven to 250°F.

Line large shallow baking sheet with aluminum foil.
Place wire rack on baking sheet. Spray with non-stick cooking spray.

2 tablespoons oregano
2 tablespoons chili powder
2 tablespoons cumin
½ teaspoon hot pepper
1 tablespoon garlic powder
1 tablespoon onion powder
1 teaspoon pepper
1 teaspoon salt

Makes about 8-10 Servings

Combine in small bowl.
Set aside and reserve.

2 racks baby back ribs
(about 2½ - 3½ pounds each)

Arrange ribs on wire rack and rub with spice mixture on both sides. Bake for 2 to 3 hours depending on size of ribs.

½ cup (1 stick) butter

Melt in large skillet.

3 cloves garlic, finely chopped
3 shallots, chopped
1 medium Vidalia onion, finely chopped

Add to skillet cook until lightly brown and tender.

1 bottle (18 ounces) smoky flavored barbecue sauce
1 cup ketchup
2 tablespoons Dijon mustard
½ cup brown sugar
1 tablespoon chili powder
1 tablespoon cumin
Salt and pepper

Preheat oven to 425°F.

Combine and pour half of mixture over ribs.

Bake, 20 to 30 minutes, or until glazed and well caramelized and browned.
Or grill on medium heat, turning and basting occasionally, about 20 minutes or until done.

To serve, slice ribs between bones and serve with reserved barbecue sauce mixture. Garnish, if desired, with chopped green onion.

TIP:

Ribs can be prepped one day ahead with dry rub seasoning. Wrap baking sheets with foil and refrigerate until ready to cook.

Caramelized,
crispy and juicy bacon with beans.
I promise this dish will be
scraped clean.

Maple Cured Baked Beans

Preheat oven to 325°F.

2 cans (16 ounces each) baked beans
¼ cup Dijon mustard
¼ cup ketchup
¼ cup maple syrup
½ cup brown sugar
1 teaspoon cumin
1 teaspoon chili powder

Combine in large bowl.

Pour into lightly greased, 9 x 13-inch baking dish or 2-quart casserole.

½ pound maple-cured bacon slices

Top with bacon.

Bake for 1 hour or until bubbly.

Makes about 10 Servings

TIP:

Can be combined two days ahead before baking.

Barley, Corn and Edamame Salad

¼ cup extra virgin olive oil

2 tablespoons white balsamic vinegar

1 lime, zested and juiced

2 cloves garlic, peeled and chopped

1 bunch cilantro or Italian parsley, chopped

1 red pepper, chopped

3 scallions, chopped

2 cups corn (fresh, canned or frozen)*

2 packages (8 ounces each),
shelled edamame

Salt and pepper to taste

Combine in large bowl and toss gently.

1 cup barley

2 cups chicken broth

1 tablespoon extra virgin olive oil

Bring to boil in medium pot.
Simmer for 30 minutes or until tender.
Drain any excess liquid.

Combine with dressing mixture.

Salt and pepper

Season.

Chill for 1 hour.

Toss before serving.

*Makes about
8 Servings*

TIPS:

*To grill corn, place ears of corn on grill
and cook 10 minutes, turning frequently.
Let cool. Slice corn kernels off the ear with
sharp knife, holding corn vertically.
Can be made one day ahead.*

*Garnish with lime wedges and
extra cilantro or parsley leaves.*

A crunchy and
colorful accompaniment.
A scrumptious salad!

Grandma's Potato Salad

Makes about
16-20 Servings

1 cup mayonnaise

¼ cup apple cider vinegar or more to taste

1 tablespoon dry mustard

3 celery stalks, coarsely chopped

3 carrots, shredded with vegetable peeler
to get nice, pretty long carrot peels

Salt and pepper

Combine in large bowl.

5 pounds russet baking potatoes*

*Boil for 10 to 15 minutes or until tender.
Peel while hot and cut into large chunks.
(Skins should peel off easily.)
Place into large bowl.
Combine with dressing mixture with
potatoes still warm.*

4 hard cooked eggs, quartered

*Reserve 1 egg, quartered. Toss remaining
quartered eggs gently with the mayonnaise
mixture and potatoes until combined.*

*Garnish with reserved quartered egg, and,
if desired, snipped chives, chopped parsley
or cooked chopped bacon.*

TIPS:

*Substitute with Red Bliss potatoes but do
not peel.*

*It's important to toss mixture with potatoes
hot. The potatoes will absorb the wonderful
flavors of the mixture.*

*When you hard cook your eggs, did you know
that old eggs peel more easily than fresh
ones? The egg yolk shrinks away from the
outer membrane near the shell, making a
little air pocket. Use eggs that have been in
your refrigerator for about one week when
hard cooking them. Peeling the hard cooked
shells will now be easy and effortless.*

*My mother-in-law, Elisa,
was an excellent cook and
created the ultimate potato salad
and homemade pizza. Here is her
version and the pizza is coming,
I promise.*

Sweet Onion Hot Dog Topping

4 large Vidalia onions,
thinly sliced (about 5 cups)

¼ cup (½ stick) butter

Cook on medium low heat in cast iron or heavy skillet for 15 to 20 minutes or until onions are golden and very caramelized.

½ cup ketchup

¼ cup brown sugar

1 teaspoon cumin

½ teaspoon cinnamon

Add to onions.

Continue to cook 5 minutes or until sugar is blended and melted.

Cool or chill until ready to use.

Makes about 2 Cups

TIP:

Can be made three days ahead and stored in refrigerator.

A childhood, late-night street snack of my husband's when he would eat dirty water dogs with onion topping from the food truck in his neighborhood of Newark, New Jersey. My husband Tommy says, "They're so good, that every time I eat them I'm 18 years old again, it's 2 o'clock in the morning and I'm with my friends on the corner of Lake Street and Bloomfield Avenue at JJ's Hotdogs."

Tri-Color Cole Slaw

1 cup mayonnaise

½ cup sour cream or plain Greek yogurt

1 tablespoon Dijon mustard

¼ cup apple cider vinegar

Salt and pepper

Combine in large bowl.

2 cups shredded green cabbage

1 cup shredded red cabbage

1 cup shredded carrots

1 cup golden or regular raisins

Add to mayonnaise mixture.

1 bunch Italian parsley, stems removed, chopped (about 1 cup)

Garnish with additional chopped parsley.

Stir in. Chill until ready to use.

Makes about 8-10 Servings

TIP:

One day ahead, mix dressing mixture and cabbage mixture separately. Day of party, mix both together and chill coleslaw up to four hours ahead of serving time.

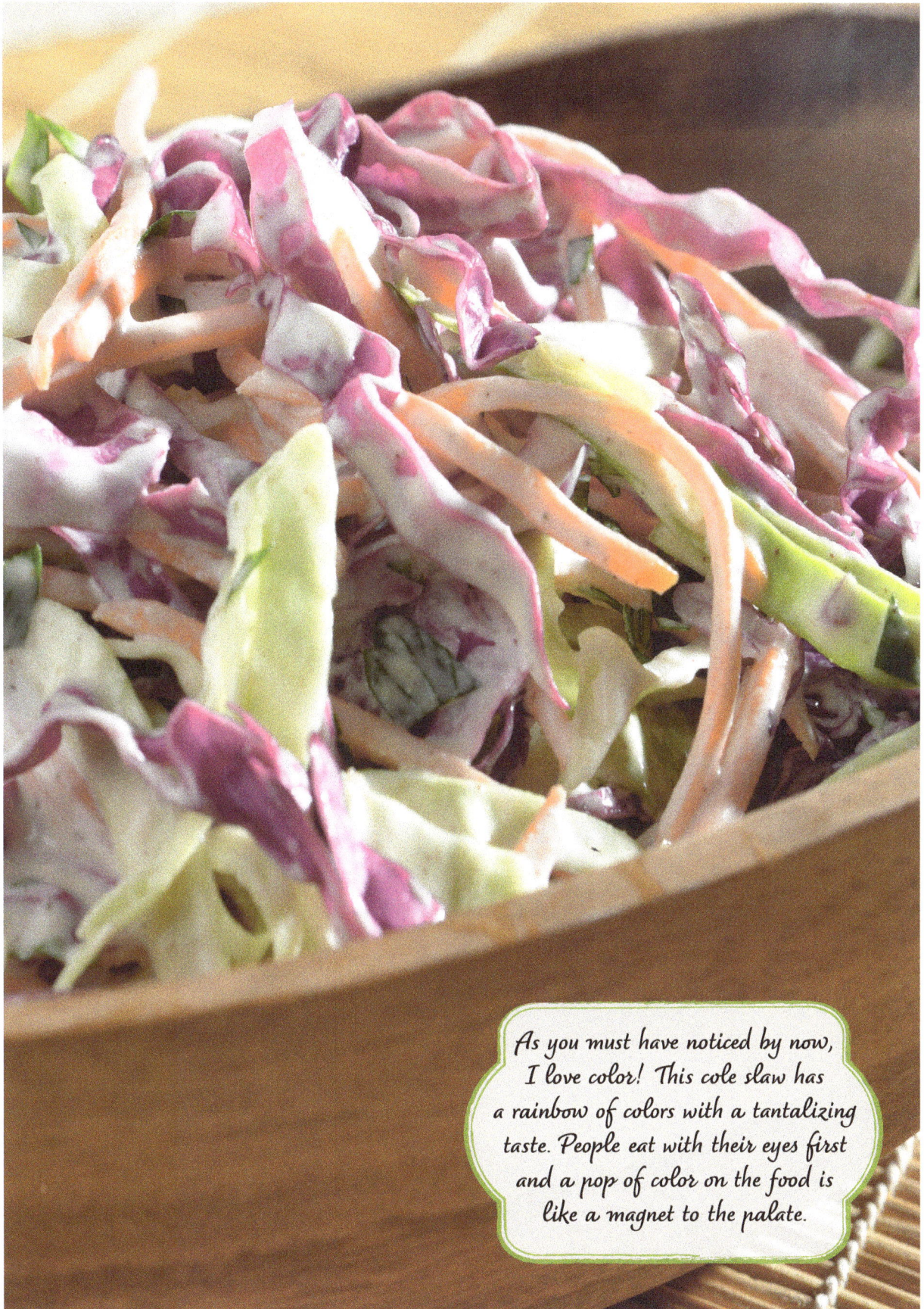

As you must have noticed by now,
I love color! This cole slaw has
a rainbow of colors with a tantalizing
taste. People eat with their eyes first
and a pop of color on the food is
like a magnet to the palate.

As a horse lover, I consider this the triple crown of chocolate brownies since it uses three textures of chocolate topped with a creamy, chocolate ganache. The added chips at the end give these brownies extra fudgy-ness.

Triple Crown Chocolate Brownies

Preheat oven to 325°F.

Line 12½ x 17½ x 1-inch half sheet baking pan with heavy-duty aluminum foil, extended over edges of pan. Spray with non-stick cooking spray, line with parchment paper and spray again. (Remember BPB: The butter, paper, butter rule in baking.) This prevents brownies from sticking to bottom of pan and create easy removal. Set aside.

2½ cups cups all-purpose flour
1 teaspoon baking soda
1 teaspoon salt

Combine in large bowl and set aside.

1½ cups sugar
2 sticks (1 cup) unsalted butter
3 tablespoons water

Combine in large saucepan. Over medium heat, bring to a boil for 1 minute or until sugar is dissolved. Remove from heat.

24 ounces semi-sweet or bittersweet chocolate squares, chopped or broken in small pieces

Add to butter mixture and stir until chocolate is melted. Let cool slightly.

6 eggs, slightly beaten
1 tablespoon vanilla extract

Add eggs to chocolate mixture, one at a time, and stir until smooth. Stir in vanilla with flour mixture and stir until smooth.

2 cups coarsely chopped walnuts or pecans (optional)

1 bag (12 ounces) semisweet or bittersweet chocolate chips

Stir into brownie mixture until smooth.

Pour into prepared pan. Bake 30 to 35 minutes. IMPORTANT NOT TO OVERBAKE. Brownies will be moist in center and do not come out clean with toothpick test. Cool. Remove entire baked brownie all at once, by lifting and holding foil edges, for easy cutting.

Top, if desired, with Chocolate Ganache* or dust with confectioner's sugar.

**Chocolate Ganache:*
In medium saucepan, over medium heat, bring 1 cup heavy cream just to a boil. Remove from heat and stir in 2 cups chopped semisweet chocolate until smooth. Pour over brownies and chill to set.

Cut brownies with long, hot, sharp knife straight down with one motion for clean, straight edges.

Makes about 4 Dozen Squares

TIPS:

The quality of the chocolate is key here so choose a rich high cocoa ratio in your chocolate such as 60% or 70% cocoa.

Can be served with or without the ganache topping. If you choose without just dust with confectioner's sugar.

Cut brownies in squares and then triangles for a different look.

These can be baked and frozen up to one month ahead. Defrost at room temperature or in refrigerator and then top with Chocolate Ganache.

Chocolate Covered Strawberries

Line two cookie sheets with parchment paper and set aside.

16 ounces chocolate, broken into small pieces or chips (use your favorite: milk, semi-sweet or dark chocolate)

Microwave in heatproof glass measuring cup or glass bowl for 1 minute. Let stand 1 minute. Stir until completely melted.

2 dozen large strawberries, washed and dried

Repeat, if necessary, every 30 seconds until chocolate is completely melted.

Dip into melted chocolate half way and place on parchment paper cookie sheets.

Chill until firm.

Makes 24 Strawberries

TIP:

For extra fun, melt white chocolate and drizzle on the dipped dark chocolate or, after dipping in chocolate, dip in finely crushed cookies or nuts.

These can be served as an easy dessert or added as a beautiful decoration to any cake or baked item.

Triple Layer Cannoli Cake
(Large Version)

Makes 36-40 Servings

Preheat oven to 350°F.

Spray 3 (14-inch) cake pans or 3 (17½ x 12½-inch half sheet pans) with non-stick cooking spray or butter. Line bottom with parchment paper and spray or butter again. (Remember BPB: The butter, paper, butter rule in baking.) This prevents baked cake from sticking to bottom of pan and create easy removal. Set aside.

This is the large party version. I have a smaller version on the following pages.

3 boxes (15.25 ounces each) cake mix*
see note below for cake mix flavor choices)

> *Prepare cakes according to package directions. Keep each mix in separate bowls.*

½ cup sour cream (makes a moister cake)

1 teaspoon vanilla extract (enhances flavor)

¼ cup rum or 1 tablespoon rum extract, (if desired in the butter cake mix)

2 tablespoons instant espresso (in devil's food cake mix)

> *Add to each flavor of prepared cake batter and blend until smooth.*
>
> *Pour into prepared pans and bake 25 minutes or until cakes test done. Let cakes cool 10 minutes and then invert on large cooling racks.*
>
> ***Freeze one hour after cakes completely cool for same day assembly. Freeze up to one month with plastic wrap for later use.*

To Assemble Cake:

1 jar (12 ounces) raspberry preserves, heated in microwave 1 minute to soften, divided

> *Place one cake on serving platter. Spread with half of raspberry preserves.*

1 container (32 ounces) whole milk ricotta***

> *Drain, 24 hours in fine strainer lined with paper towels or cheesecloth. Straining ricotta removes water so cannoli cream is thick.*

*1½ cups confectioner's sugar

1 teaspoon vanilla extract

> *Combine in large bowl of electric mixer with strained ricotta. Beat until smooth.*

1 bag (12 ounces) mini semi-sweet chocolate chips

> *Stir into ricotta mixture.*
> *Spread mixture evenly onto cake.*
> *Top with second cake.*
> *Spread with remaining raspberry preserves.*

96

2 boxes (3.9 ounces each)
chocolate fudge instant pudding

2 cups (1 pint) whole milk

2 cups (1 pint) heavy cream

2 tablespoons instant espresso

1 teaspoon vanilla extract

Mix in large bowl of electric mixer.
Let sit for 5 minutes or until thickened.

Spread on cake.
Note: May have a little left over on round cakes.

2 bananas, thinly sliced

Top with bananas.
Top with third cake.

6 cups heavy cream

3 cups confectioner's sugar

1 tablespoon vanilla extract

In large chilled bowl of electric mixer with whisk attachment, whip cream on medium high speed until it starts to thicken. Reduce speed to low and slowly add confectioner's sugar and vanilla. Increase speed to high and whip until stiff peaks. Reserve 4 cups whipped cream to decorate. Spread remaining whipped cream on sides and top of cake. Pipe top and bottom edges of cake using large star tip for a finished look, as desired.

1½ cups sliced almonds, toasted (optional)

Gently pat sides of cake with almonds, if desired.

Strawberries for garnish

Garnish with Chocolate Covered Strawberries (See page 94).

When we were growing up, Mom always bought our birthday cakes at Rispoli's Italian Bakery in Ridgefield Park, New Jersey. I just had to make one that was comparable when we had birthday parties for my girls. This version is pretty close and requested at all celebrations! You can make a scratch cake, my favorite is a genoise-type, but this is the shortcut version. You won't have a piece leftover, I promise!

TIPS:

* For black and white cake layers, either use 2 devil's food cakes mixes and 1 butter cake mix or 2 butter cake mixes and 1 devil's food cake mix.

**One day before the party, assemble with cakes frozen (so much easier to handle). Finish with assembly and garnish as above. Keep refrigerated until ready to serve.

***To avoid straining, substitue whole milk ricotta with ricotta impastata found in specialty Italian or restaurant supply stores.

Ask supermarket for recommendation. 97

Triple Layer Cannoli Cake
(Small Version)

Preheat oven to 350°F.

Spray 2 (9-inch) cake pans with non-stick cooking spray or butter.
Line bottom with circle of parchment paper and spray or butter again.
(Remember BPB: The butter, paper, butter rule in baking.) This prevents baked cake from
sticking to bottom of pan and create easy removal. Set aside.

1 box (15.25 ounces) devil's food cake mix
1 box (15.25 ounces) butter cake mix

Mix cakes according to package directions.
Keep each mix in separate bowls.

½ cup sour cream (makes a moister cake)

1 teaspoon vanilla extract (enhances flavor)

¼ cup rum or 1 tablespoon rum extract,
(if desired in the butter cake mix)

2 tablespoons instant espresso
(in devil's food cake mix)

Add to each flavor of prepared cake batter
and blend until smooth.

Pour into prepared pans and bake
20 minutes or until cakes test done. Let
cakes cool 10 minutes and then invert on
large cooling racks.

*Freeze for one hour after cakes completely
cool for same day assembly. Freeze up to one
month with plastic wrap for later use.

Slice each cake horizontally in half to make
2 layers. You will have now 2 layers devil's
food and 2 layers butter cake to alternate
layers of cake to your liking so it appears
black and white. (Note: You will have one
layer left over and save for another use.)**

To Assemble Cake:

6 tablespoons raspberry preserves, heated
in microwave 1 minute to soften, divided

Place one cake on serving platter. Spread
with half of raspberry preserves.

1 container (15 ounces) whole milk ricotta***

Drain, 24 hours in fine strainer lined with
paper towels or cheesecloth. Straining ricotta
removes water so cannoli cream is thick.

1½ cups confectioner's sugar

1 teaspoon vanilla extract

Combine in large bowl of electric mixer with
strained ricotta. Beat until smooth.

98

1 bag (12 ounces) mini semi-sweet chocolate chips

Stir into ricotta mixture. Spread mixture evenly onto cake. Top with second cake. Spread with remaining raspberry preserves.

1 box (3.9 ounces) chocolate fudge instant pudding
1 cup whole milk
1 cup heavy cream
1 tablespoon instant espresso
½ teaspoon vanilla extract

Mix in large bowl of electric mixer. Let sit for 5 minutes or until thickened. Spread on cake. (Note: May have a little left over on round cakes.)

1 banana, thinly sliced

Top with bananas.
Top with third cake.

3 cups heavy cream
1½ cups additional confectioner's sugar
1 teaspoon vanilla extract

In large chilled bowl of electric mixer with whisk attachment, whip cream on medium high speed until it starts to thicken. Reduce speed to low and slowly add confectioner's sugar and vanilla. Increase speed to high and whip until stiff peaks.

Reserve 2 cup whipped cream to decorate. Spread remaining whipped cream on sides and top of cake. Pipe top and bottom edges of cake using large star tip for a finished look, as desired.

1 cup sliced almonds, toasted (optional)**

Gently pat sides of cake with almonds, if desired.

Strawberries for garnish

Garnish with Chocolate Covered Strawberries (see page 94).

Garnish with Chocolate Covered Strawberries (see page 94).

TIPS:

*One day before the party, assemble with cakes frozen (so much easier to handle). Finish with assembly and garnish as above. Keep refrigerated until ready to serve.

**If desired, crumb extra cake layer and use to decorate side of cake instead of almonds.

***To avoid straining, substitue whole milk ricotta with ricotta impastata found in specialty Italian or restaurant supply stores.

Italian night

Italian Sunday 'Gravy' Dinner

Antipasti
Tri-Color Roasted Peppers
Grilled Eggplant with Rosemary
Marinated Chickpeas with Lemon and Oregano
Sautéed Spinach with Pignoli Nuts

Fresh Mozzarella *with* Tomato and Basil

Italian-Style Sunday 'Gravy'

Italian Meatballs

Braciole

Nana's Stuffed Artichokes

Tiramisu Cheesecake

Pignoli Cookies

Citrus Biscotti

Limoncello

Roasted peppers
are a staple on
my antipasti tray.
Usually I use three
or four colors
of peppers.

Tri-Color Roasted Peppers

Makes about 2 Cups

Preheat oven to broil.

8 peppers (colors of your choice) }

Place on large baking sheet.

Broil, turning occasionally, for 10 minutes, or until pepper skin is charred and blackened.

Place peppers in paper bag and fold top to keep it tightly closed. This allows peppers to steam and makes it easier to peel skins. Allow to cool, 20 minutes.

Peel skins off peppers under slowly running water with strainer underneath. Remove stems and seeds as well.

Place cleaned peppers on paper towels to drain. (At this point they can be put in large plastic bag or plastic container.)

½ cup extra virgin olive oil

4 cloves garlic, chopped }

Combine in 2-cup heatproof glass measuring cup. Microwave for 1 minute (or heat mixture in small saucepan over low heat, 3 minutes). This will make garlic sweeter, removing bitterness and infusing olive oil with flavor. I make a big batch of this mixture and use it for most of my antipasti preparation. This mixture can stay in the refrigerator up to one week.

3 tablespoons white balsamic vinegar

4 cloves garlic, chopped

1 cup fresh basil leaves, rolled and sliced thin

Salt and pepper }

Toss with peppers.

TIPS:

These also make delicious toppers for sandwiches and salads.

They can be stored in refrigerator up to three days or frozen up to one month.

105

Grilled Eggplant *with* Rosemary

Preheat oven to 400°F.

2 tablespoons extra virgin olive oil } *Drizzle on large baking sheet.*

1 large eggplant, unpeeled,
sliced into ⅛-inch crosswise slices } *Place eggplant slices in single layer.
(Use two sheet pans if necessary so they
do not overlap.)*

½ cup extra virgin olive oil

4 cloves garlic, finely chopped

4 sprigs fresh rosemary stems
(about 4-inches long), leaves
removed and chopped slightly

Salt and pepper

} *Combine in 2-cup heatproof glass
measuring cup. Microwave for 1 minute
(or heat mixture in small saucepan over
low heat, 3 minutes). This will make garlic
sweeter, removing bitterness and infusing
olive oil with flavor. I make a big batch
of this mixture and use it for most of my
antipasti preparation. This mixture can
stay in the refrigerator up to one week.
Drizzle infused oil on eggplant slices.*

Salt and pepper } *Season eggplant.*

Bake 15 minutes or until tender.

Let cool.

Serve at room temperature.

*So savory and satisfying,
the rosemary complements the
earthiness of the eggplant.*

TIPS:

*Use the leftovers on sandwiches and
salads, too.*

*This can be made three days ahead and
stored in the refrigerator.*

Marinated Chickpeas
with Lemon and Oregano

Makes about 3 Cups

½ cup extra virgin olive oil

2 cloves garlic, chopped

Salt and pepper

} *Combine in 2-cup heatproof glass measuring cup. Microwave for 1 minute (or heat mixture in small saucepan over low heat, 3 minutes). This will make garlic sweeter, removing bitterness and infusing olive oil with flavor. I make a big batch of this mixture and use it for most of my antipasti preparation. This mixture can stay in the refrigerator up to one week.*

2 cans (15.3 ounces each) chickpeas (garbanzo beans) drained

2 lemons zested and juiced

1 tablespoon fresh oregano, chopped

Salt and pepper

} *Combine in large bowl with olive oil mixture.*

Marinate at least 2 hours or overnight.

Serve at room temperature.

TIP:

This can be made two days ahead.

I absolutely love chickpeas, also known as garbanzo beans. Oregano and lemon give this dish its unique essence.

Sautéed Spinach *with* Pignoli Nuts

½ cup pignoli nuts (pine nuts) } *Toast in large skillet until golden. Remove and set aside.*

4 tablespoons extra virgin olive oil, divided

4 cloves garlic, chopped, divided } *Add half of olive oil and half of garlic in same skillet on medium heat. Cook until garlic is fragrant, about 2 minutes.*

2 containers (1 pound each) fresh baby spinach } *Add half and cook on medium heat until spinach just starts to wilt. Do not overcook or will be too watery.*

Salt and pepper } *Season spinach mixture.*

Place in serving bowl.

Repeat with remaining ingredients.

Combine both batches and stir in pignoli nuts.

Add to serving bowl.

Serve at room temperature.

Makes about 8 Servings

When I serve this as an antipasto, it's the first to disappear.

TIPS:

This dish should be prepared no more than about one hour ahead to prevent it from becoming watery.

Double this recipe because it's always the most popular antipasto.

If you have leftovers, they are terrific for a frittata the next morning.

Fresh Mozzarella *with* Tomato and Basil

1 ball (1 pound) fresh mozzarella,
cut into ¼-inch slices

3 large New Jersey beefsteak or
6 plum tomatoes, cut into ¼-inch slices

} *Arrange on platter alternating the slices.*

¼ cup extra virgin olive oil
Salt and pepper

} *Drizzle and sprinkle on platter.*

12 to 16 fresh basil leaves

} *Top and serve at room temperature.*

Makes 12-16 Servings

TIP:
*Never chill freshly made mozzarella.
Buy it on the day you plan to serve it,
and keep it at room temperature.*

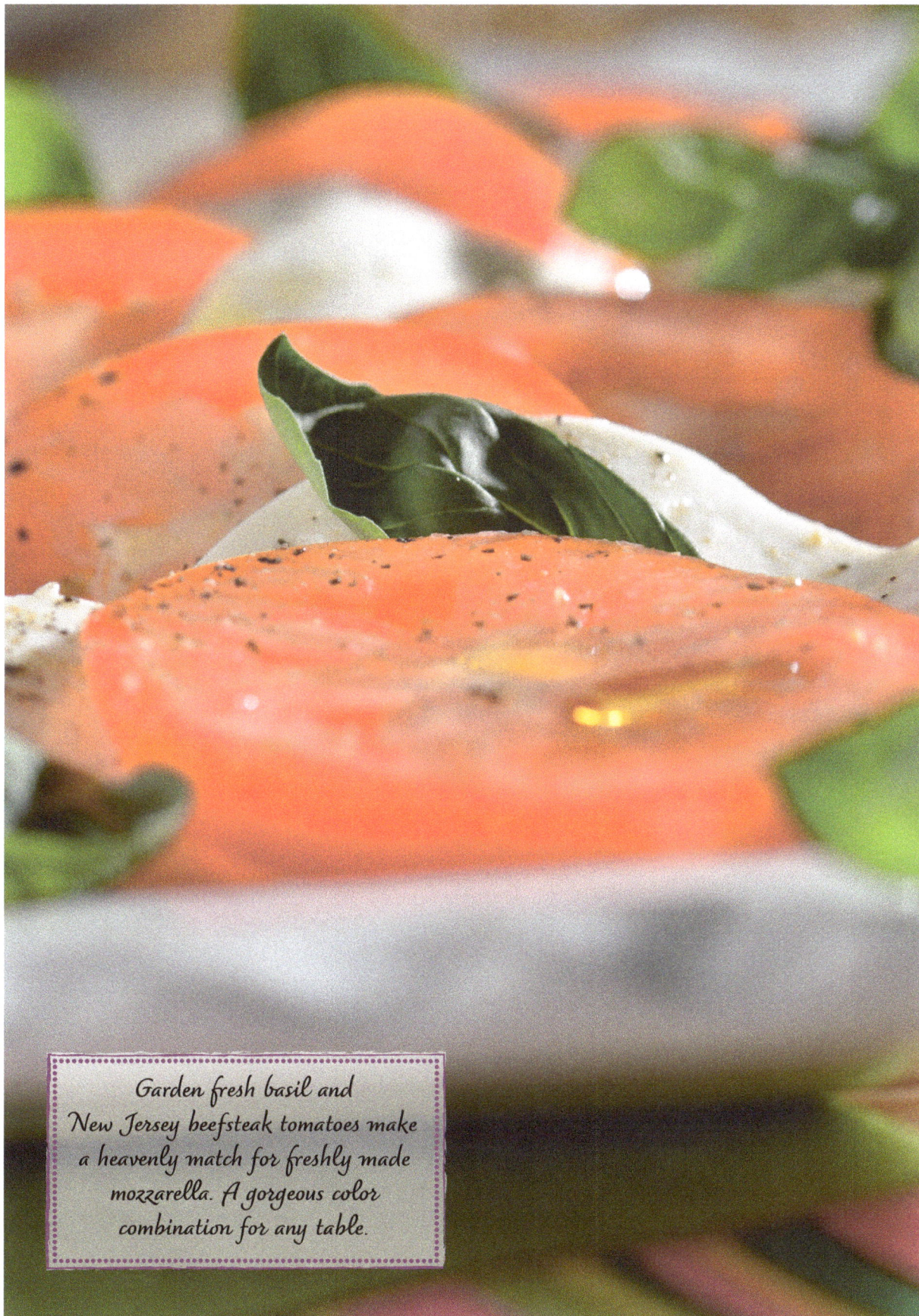

Garden fresh basil and
New Jersey beefsteak tomatoes make
a heavenly match for freshly made
mozzarella. A gorgeous color
combination for any table.

"Gravy," the term for the
Italian American version for red meat sauce,
is our three generation family tradition. It's
slow cooking and full of wholesome Italian
ingredients, making the most tantalizing
fragrance in your home all day long.

Italian-Style Sunday 'Gravy'

3 to 4 tablespoons extra virgin olive oil 4 cloves garlic, finely chopped 1 large carrot, chopped* 1 medium onion, chopped	Heat large stock pot. Add olive oil. Then, add vegetables and cook over medium heat, 5 minutes or until soft.
½ can (from a 6 ounce can) tomato paste	Add to stock pot and cook another 5 minutes, stirring occasionally, until blended.
¼ cup full-bodied red wine	Add to stock pot and cook until evaporated and smooth, about another 5 minutes.
2 cans (6 pounds each) San Marzano Italian peeled tomatoes	Add tomatoes to stock pot and blend with immersion blender until pureed (or puree in blender).
6 sweet Italian sausage links (about 2 pounds) 1 piece (8 ounces) boneless pork loin, pork neck bones or pork ribs 1 piece (8 ounces) boneless eye round, sirloin steak, or boneless beef steak 6 braciole (see page 116)	Cook in large skillet, one meat at a time, over medium heat, 5 to 10 minutes or until browned. Place into prepared sauce. (NOTE: add more red wine and let evaporate, deglaze, if desired).
4 to 5 fresh basil leaves Salt and pepper	Add to stock pot and let simmer (slight bubbles should break surface), 3 hours, stirring occasionally, on low heat. Watch sauce carefully so it does not burn.
48-50 Meatballs (see page 115)	Add meatballs and let simmer, for 1 more hour.

TIPS:

*Carrot gives just enough natural sweetness and rounds out the sauce flavor.

Can be stored in airtight containers up to one week or frozen up to three months.

Recipe can be easily halved or doubled.

Remove all meat and serve.

Serve with cavatelli, penne or your favorite pasta, ricotta pot cheese and grated Parmesan cheese.

Makes about 25 Servings

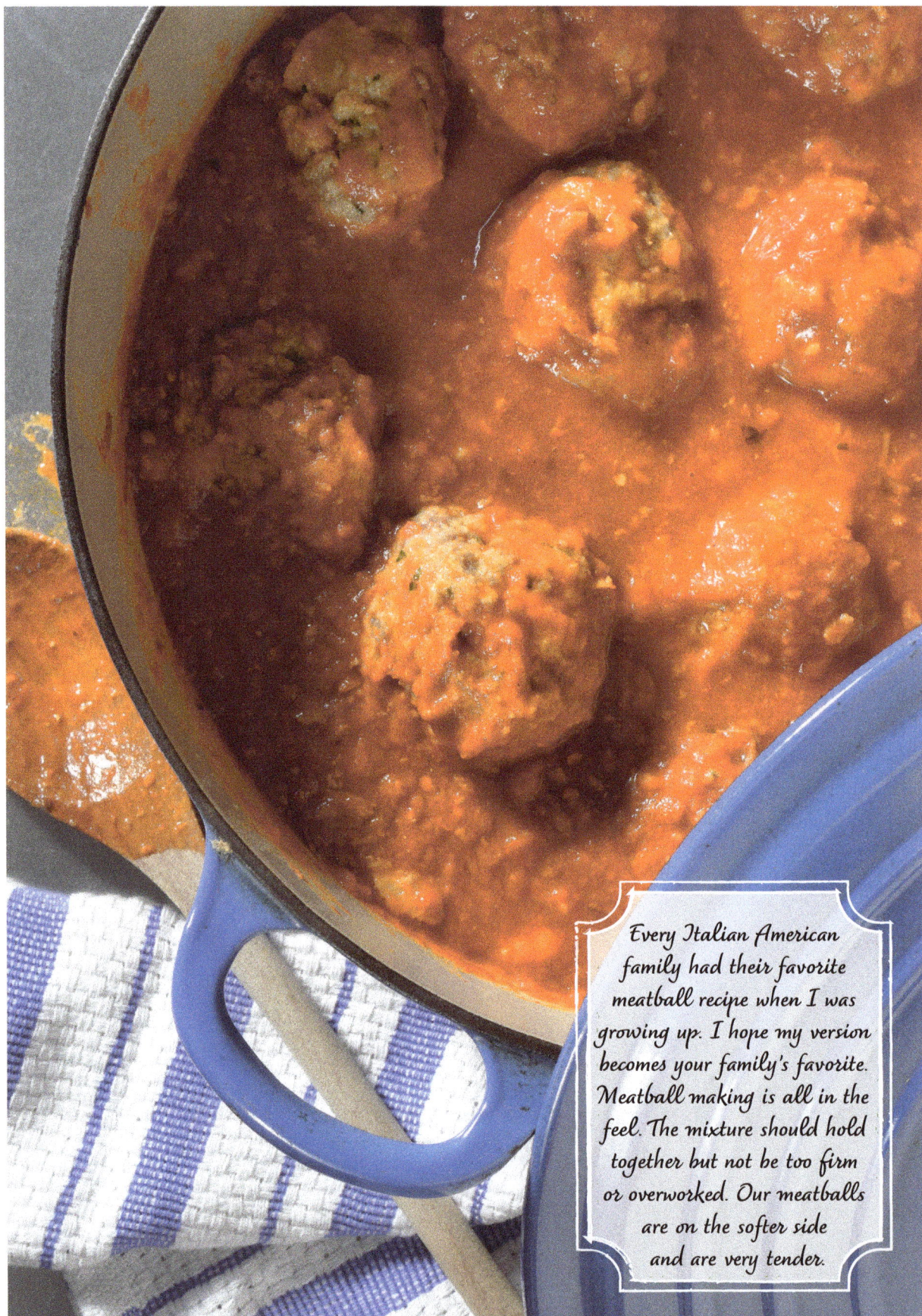

Every Italian American family had their favorite meatball recipe when I was growing up. I hope my version becomes your family's favorite. Meatball making is all in the feel. The mixture should hold together but not be too firm or overworked. Our meatballs are on the softer side and are very tender.

Italian Meatballs

1 large Italian-style bread,
about 1½ pounds, or any good quality
Italian bread, torn into small pieces*

1 to 1½ cup water or milk

Add bread in large bowl.
Add a little water or milk at a time, and squeeze with hands until very soft, wet and blended (pastelike but not watery).

4 cloves garlic, finely chopped

6 to 8 large eggs

4 pounds ground meatloaf mix
(pork, veal, beef)

1 cup grated Parmesan cheese

1 cup grated Pecorino Romano cheese

1 bunch Italian parsley, stems removed,
finely chopped

Drizzle of olive oil

Salt and pepper

Add all ingredients to bowl and drizzle with olive oil.

Mix for at least 10 minutes with hands until well blended and mixture is soft but holds together when rolled. (NOTE: Start with lesser amount of eggs and add maximum amount only if mixture feels too stiff. A great test to make sure texture and seasoning is correct is to roll a small meatball, cook it until done and then taste. If meatball tastes to your liking and holds together but still tender you are all set to continue. This is a perfect way to correct seasoning and texture before you cook them.) Roll meatballs into 2½ to 3-inch sized balls.

Makes 48 - 50 Meatballs

Canola oil for frying.

*Fill large, deep heavy skillet 1-inch depth with canola oil. Drizzle with splash of extra virgin olive oil. Cook meatballs on medium high heat in single layer (DO NOT OVERCROWD), about 5 minutes per side or until browned and done in center. **Fry in batches. Drain on paper towel-lined sheet pan. You won't be able to resist eating one before they make it to the gravy!*

TIPS:

Use stale or defrosted frozen bread if desired.

**Meatballs can also be baked and are just as delicious. Place rolled meatballs on parchment-lined baking sheet drizzled with olive oil. Bake at 350°F, 30 minutes or until cooked through.*
Continue as above for the gravy.

Can be refrigerated in airtight containers up to one week or frozen up to three months to enjoy easily every Sunday.

Good rule of thumb is 1 pound of meat yields 12 meatballs. Recipe can be easily doubled, or even tripled, for a big batch of meatball fun.

Add meatballs to gravy (see page 113) for last hour of cooking.

Braciole

1½ to 2 pounds beef top round,
very thinly sliced (about 8 slices)

Coarse salt and black pepper

} *Season meat.*

8 slices (around 4 ounces) prosciutto

} *Top each slice of meat with slice of prosciutto.*

1½ cups fresh bread crumbs,
or more if needed

½ cup milk or water, or more if needed

Salt and pepper

} *Moisten bread crumbs in medium bowl with milk until mixture holds together when squeezed.*

1 cup grated Parmesan cheese

1 small onion, finely chopped

2 cloves garlic, finely chopped

1 cup Italian parsley leaves, stems removed

} *Add to crumbs and combine well.*

Spread thin layer of stuffing down center of each beef slice and roll tightly.

Fasten rolled meat with wooden toothpicks or tie with butcher's string.

2 tablespoons extra virgin olive oil

2 cloves garlic, finely chopped

} *Cook over medium heat in large skillet, 1 minute or until garlic is fragrant.*
Brown meat on all sides, about 5 minutes.

Place braciole and juices into Italian-Style Sunday Gravy (see page 113).
Allow to simmer for at least 3 hours or until tender.

Slice and serve with Italian-Style Sunday Gravy, meats and meatballs.

*Makes
8 Servings*

TIP:

Can be stored in airtight containers up to one week or frozen up to three months.

This traditional Italian meat specialty completes your Sunday Gravy extravaganza.

I videoed my Nana when she was in her late 80's, showing me how to make these artichokes. I asked her, "Nana, how do you know how much bread to use?" She replied, "How many people are you having?" I said, "Ten." She began to grab handfuls of bread stuffing counting to ten. The stuffing filled ten medium artichokes perfectly! It was a useful lesson learned for measuring.

Nana's Stuffed Artichokes

2 lemons, halved (prevents browning)

Fill large stockpot two thirds with water. Add lemons and a bring to a boil.

12 medium artichokes, leaves trimmed and stems removed (reserve stems)

Add and cook 10 to 12 minutes (depending on size) or until the leaves pull off easily. Drain and let cool.

5 cups fresh breadcrumbs (Italian or Semolina bread, processed in food processer until fine)*

1 cup panko breadcrumbs

½ cup grated Parmesan cheese

½ cup grated Pecorino Romano cheese

1 bunch Italian parsley, chopped

½ cup extra virgin olive oil

6 cloves garlic, peeled and finely chopped

Salt and pepper

Combine. (If too dry, add a little more olive oil. Mixture should hold together slightly.) Fill center and outside leaves of artichokes with breadcrumb mixture. Distribute mixture evenly.

Preheat oven to 350°F.

2 cups Chicken Stock broth (see page 94), or water

½ cup extra-virgin olive oil

6 cloves garlic, peeled and thinly sliced

In a large shallow baking pan, add reserved stems, salt and pepper. Place artichokes in prepared pan standing upright. Loosely cover with aluminum foil. Bake, 20 minutes or until tender and heated through.

Baste occasionally, about every 5 minutes, during cooking time. Remove foil. Broil, 5 minutes or until browned and crispy. Enjoy with juice from roasting pan for dipping.

TIPS:

*Can substitute Panko or plain dried breadcrumbs.

Always use small to medium sizes. If you can only find large artichokes, make sure to blanch them until the leaves pull off easily before you stuff them.

Artichokes can be stuffed one day ahead.

You can also double the chicken stock juice and serve heated with the artichokes for extra dipping.

Makes 12 Artichokes

Tiramisu Cheesecake

Preheat oven to 350°F.

Place shallow baking pan on lower rack in oven (half sheet pan works perfectly) and fill with at least 1-inch water. The moisture from the steam helps prevent the cheesecake from cracking.

Open springform pan. Insert the bottom pan upside down and close springform pan.
Line 9-inch springform pan with circle of parchment paper.
This method allows your cheesecake to slide right off onto your serving plate much easier.
Wrap outside of springform with heavy-duty aluminum foil to prevent
any seeping of butter through pan when baking.

Crust:

Makes about 16 Servings

40 vanilla cookies, finely crushed (about 2 cups crumbs)

½ cup (1 stick) butter, melted

2 tablespoons sugar

1 teaspoon cinnamon

Combine in small bowl. Press mixture firmly into bottom of prepared springform pan.

Bake, 8 minutes. Cool.

Filling:

4 packages (8 ounces each) cream cheese, softened

1½ cups sugar

Combine in large bowl of electric mixer. Beat on high speed until light and fluffy, about 5 minutes.

1 cup mascarpone cheese or sour cream

Add to mixture and beat on medium speed until smooth.

4 eggs

Add eggs one at a time and beat on low speed just until smooth, about 1 to 2 minutes. DO NOT OVERBEAT. This also helps prevent cheesecake from craking.

2 tablespoons instant espresso mixed with ⅓ cup hot water

1 teaspoon vanilla extract

2 squares (1 ounce each) semi-sweet chocolate, chopped, or ½ cup mini semi-sweet chocolate chips

Add and beat on low speed until smooth. Pour batter into prepared pan. Place on middle rack of oven. Bake 1 hour and 30 minutes or until center is almost set. Turn oven off. Let cool in the oven for 30 minutes. Chill 3 hours or overnight.

TIP:
Serve with whipped cream, chocolate shavings and cocoa powder.

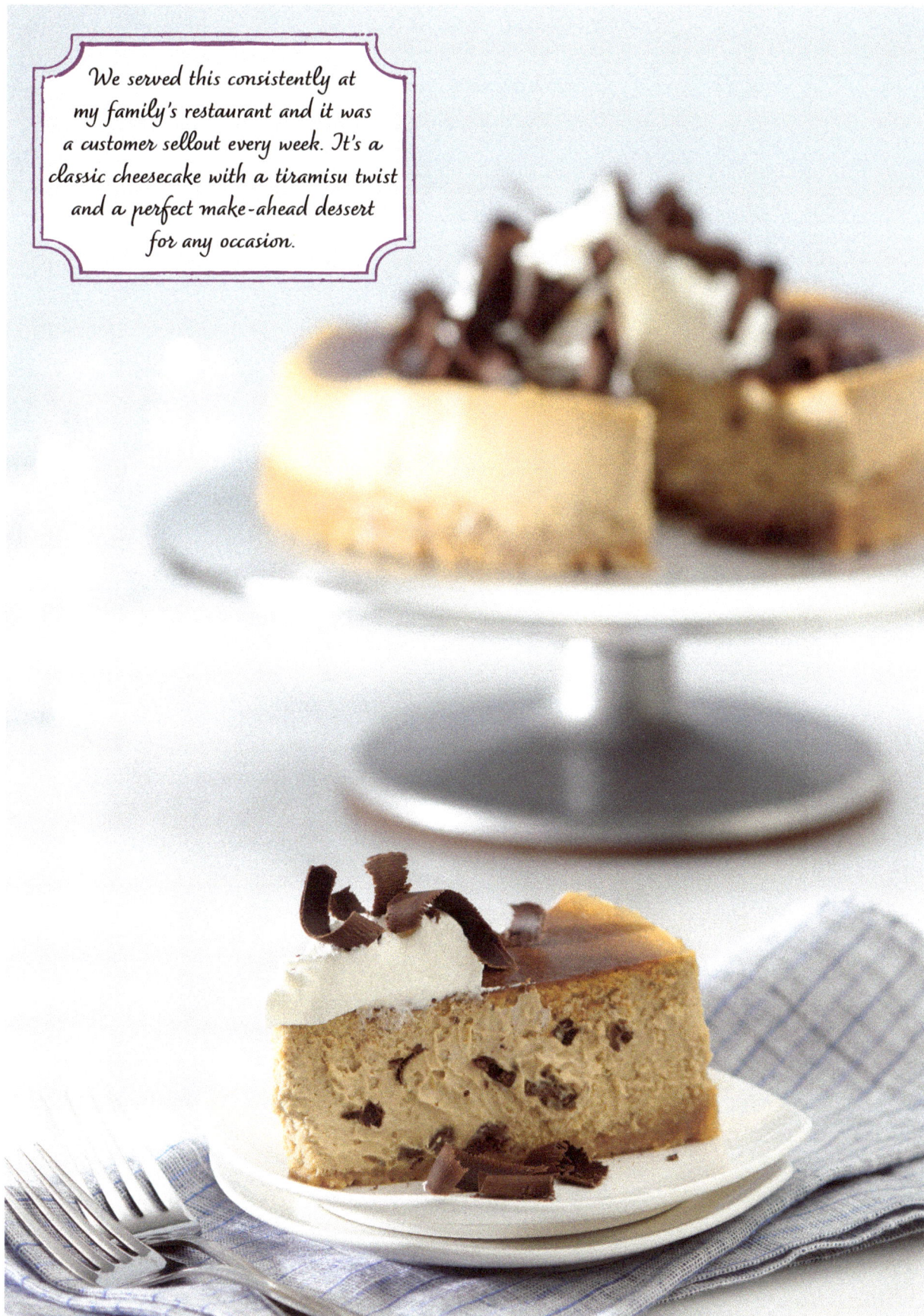

Pignoli Cookies

Preheat oven to 325°F.
Line baking sheets with baking parchment paper.

12 ounces almond paste*
½ cup sugar
1 cup confectioner's sugar

} *Combine in food processor. Process until smooth, or sand-like consistency.*

2 egg whites
½ teaspoon almond extract

} *Add to large bowl of electric mixer. Beat on high speed until stiff.*

Fold in almond/sugar mixture.

1¼ cup pignoli nuts (pine nuts)

} *Place on flat plate.*

Using 1½-inch ice cream scooper or tablespoon, roll balls into nuts to completely cover. Place 2-inches apart onto prepared baking sheets and slightly flatten.

Bake, 15 to 18 minutes or until slightly golden.

Cool on wire racks.

Makes about 2 Dozen Cookies

TIPS:

*Purchase canned almond paste from your local baker for best results. The fresher the almond paste the softer the cookies.

If desired, sprinkle with confectioner's sugar.

Can be stored in airtight container for one week or freeze up to one month.

Recipe can easily be doubled (which I highly recommend).

These traditional Italian cookies are crisp on the outside and chewy on the inside. It's the cookie that everyone steals from the cookie tray first.

Citrus Biscotti

Preheat oven to 350°F.
Line baking sheets with parchment paper.

4 cups unbleached all-purpose flour
2 tablespoons baking powder
2 teaspoons salt

Combine in medium bowl. Set aside.

2 cups (4 sticks) unsalted butter, softened
2 cups sugar

Combine in large bowl of electric mixer. Beat on high speed until light and fluffy, about 5 minutes.

8 large eggs
1 teaspoon vanilla extract
1 lemon, zested
1 orange, zested

Combine in large glass measuring cup or bowl. Add slowly to butter mixture on low speed (batter will look curdled). Increase to medium speed. Beat for 1 minute.

Makes about 10 Dozen Cookies

Slowly add flour mixture to egg mixture on low speed until combined. Beat until smooth, about 2 minutes. DO NOT CHILL!

Fill large pastry bag with batter (no tip, just make 1-inch opening). Squeeze batter onto baking sheets into two parallel lines, about 3-inches apart (batter will spread when baking). If bigger cookies are desired, make wider strips of batter but only make one line in center of baking sheet.

TIPS:

This recipe can be easily halved.

Add 1 cup of your favorite nuts, toasted and chopped to batter mixture before baking.

Can substitute citrus zest with 1 tablespoon anise extract.

Can be made and stored in airtight container for two weeks or frozen for two month.

Bake, 8 to 10 minutes or until lightly golden. Let cool a few minutes.

Loosen cookie strips underneath using offset metal spatula. Using sharp serrated knife, slice on diagonal into ½-inch slices. Turn cookies on their side and bake additional 5 to 7 minutes or until a light golden color.

Let cool. Dust with generous amounts of confectioners' sugar.

With the inspiration of my Nana's biscotti and a collection of friends' and relatives' recipes, along with my own testing, I created this delicate biscotti which can become one of your treasures. This citrus combination defies you to eat just one!

Limoncello is an Italian liqueur made from lemons. It originated from Italy's Amalfi Coast (Capri, Sorrento and Liguria) from their famously huge lemons. It's served ice cold from the freezer as an aperitif or after dinner.

This recipe has brought together many treasured lifelong friendships at our home celebrations, restaurant and other numerous occasions. I make a double batch (a case of lemons usually has around 90 lemons) and start my batches in the summer. It also makes a perfect, elegant gift that will definitely impress, especially during the holidays.

Limoncello

2 bottles (750 milliliter each) 90 proof, good quality grain alcohol

1 bottle (1.75 liters) or 2 bottles (750 milliliters each) 80 proof, good quality vodka

Pour all alcohol in large gallon-type glass jars (found in kitchen supply stores or sun tea jars work great, too).

45 large lemons (scrubbed and washed)

Using a potato/vegetable peeler or paring knife, carefully peel off just the yellow skin of lemons. It's very important the white part under the peel (also known as white pith) is removed underneath the lemon peels, or else this will make mixture bitter. Make peels as large as possible to make it easier later when straining. Place peels in alcohol.

Cover tightly and store in cool (not cold) dark place so alcohol can extract oils from peels to create infusion.

Allow to sit for at least three weeks to three months. Stir gently every few days. The longer the lemon peels sit, the better the color and flavor. A good test is to take one lemon peel and see if it snaps when you bend it. If it does, it's ready.

6 cups bottled or distilled water

8 cups sugar

Bring to a boil in large saucepan over medium high heat and simmer, about 5 to 10 minutes or until sugar is completely dissolved. Let cool completely.

Strain lemon mixture into another large gallon-type glass container using a large, fine, mesh strainer and large coffee filters. (This takes time and is a little messy.) Repeat straining process.

Add cooled syrup to strained alcohol and see limoncello come to life as it turns a bright yellow color. At this point, pour limoncello into pretty glass bottles with cork tops.

Return to cool, dry place for at least another two weeks. After two weeks, keep in freezer for three to six months.

TIPS:

It's terrific as a cordial served with my Citrus Biscotti (see page 124) after dinner and delicious over vanilla ice cream.

Start saving glass bottles from any home decorating store early, making sure that the tops are airtight. The corks can also be waxed closed, if desired, to make sure they are well-sealed.

Game Day Fun

Mini Hot Dog Crescents

Onion Dip

'Super' Muffaletta Sandwich

Hot 'n Spicy BBQ Chicken Wings

Quarterback Pulled Pork Sliders

Sweet Potato Steak Fries

Macho Nachos

Savory Spicy Salsa

Mango Salsa *with* Cinnamon Pita Chips

Stromboli

Meatball Parmesan Subs

Grandma's Pizza

'Big Blue' Berry Lemon Zested Pound Cake

New York-Style Cheesecake

Can't have a party without the old time favorite of pigs in a blanket! Kids love them but adults will, too!

Mini Hot Dog Crescents

Preheat oven to 375°F.
Line baking sheet with parchment paper.

1 can (8 ounces)
refrigerated crescent rolls

Unroll crescent dough and separate into 8 triangles. Cut each triangle in half.

16 cocktail wieners or your favorite
hot dog, cut into 16 2-inch pieces

Place 1 wiener on longest side of each triangle; roll up and place, point side down, on prepared cookie sheet.

Bake, 11 to 15 minutes or until deep golden brown.

Remove immediately from cookie sheet.

Serve with ketchup, mustard and/or relish.

Makes
16 Appetizers

TIP:

Insert your favorite cheese,
if desired, before rolling for extra fun.

Onion Dip

1 pint (2 cups) sour cream or
plain Greek yogurt

1 envelope dried onion soup mix

1 tablespoon minced dried onion flakes

1 tablespoon minced dried garlic

1 teaspoon onion powder

Combine in small bowl.

Chill, 2 hours.

*Serve with your favorite assorted dippers
and potato chips.*

*Makes
2 Cups*

TIP:
*Can be made two days ahead to blend the
flavor of onions.*

*My husband's request at every party!
Even though there would be so many
appetizers, everyone likes the classic
onion dip, and, of course, served
with salty potato chips.
An oldie but goodie!*

'Super' Muffaletta Sandwich

Makes 16 Servings

1 jar (10 ounces) Manzanilla olives (stuffed pimento olives), drained and finely chopped

1 jar (9.5 ounces) pitted Kalamata olives, drained and finely chopped

1 jar (6 ounces) pitted black olives, drained and finely chopped

1 jar (3.5 ounces) small capers, drained and chopped

2 cloves garlic, chopped

2 tablespoons white wine or white balsamic vinegar

2 tablespoons extra virgin olive oil

¼ cup chopped Italian parsley

Salt and pepper

Combine in large bowl.
Set aside. Can be made two days ahead.

1 large round Italian bread

Slice Italian bread in half horizontally. Hollow out bottom slightly, add olive mixture and spread over bottom.

4 ounces sliced soppressata

3 ounces sliced capicola

4 ounces sliced salami

8 ounces sliced smoked ham

8 ounces sliced provolone

1 pound sliced fresh mozzarella

1 jar (8 ounces) roasted peppers, drained and sliced

2 cups arugula

Layer and cover with reserved top.

Can be made one day ahead. Keep wrapped in refrigerator, at least 2 hours.

To serve, slice into wedges.

This traditional Sicilian sandwich made with a round Italian soft loaf filled with Italian cold cuts and this scrumptious olive salad originated in New Orleans. Here is my version that's served at all our tailgates, playoff and Super Bowl games for the Giants!

TIP:

Wrap tightly so bread is compressed slightly and then easily sliced into wedges.

Hot 'n Spicy BBQ Chicken Wings

Preheat oven to 450°F.

Line 15 x 10½-inch baking pan with heavy-duty aluminum foil and spray with non-stick cooking spray.

1 jar (18 ounces) barbecue sauce

3 tablespoons chili powder

1 teaspoon ground cumin

¼ cup hot pepper sauce

Combine in medium bowl and set aside.

2 packages (about 1½ pounds each) chicken wingettes *

Salt and pepper

Add to prepared pan.

Bake 20 minutes, turning once.

Pour prepared barbecue sauce mixture over chicken and stir to coat.

Bake additional 20 minutes or until crisp.

Makes 12 Servings

Gorgonzola Dip

1 cup sour cream

¼ cup mayonnaise

2 tablespoons Dijon mustard

1 cup crumbled gorgonzola

Salt and pepper

Combine in small bowl.
Makes about 1½ cups.

Hot 'n Spicy but served with a creamy Gorgonzola Dip to cool off your palate.

A twist to Buffalo wings without the frying.

TIPS:

* You can use regular chicken wings, cut in half. Remove wing tips.

Substitute plain Greek yogurt for sour cream and blue cheese for gorgonzola.

The slow cooker has been underestimated for years and has made an enormous popular comeback. Try this slow cooker delight that you combine quickly, and letting it do all the work. Your football fans will love this one! A make-ahead the morning before or plug in the day of ready for game time.

Quarterback Pulled Pork Sliders

1 large sweet Vidalia onion, sliced
2 garlic cloves, peeled

} *Add to bottom of slow cooker.*

*Makes
6-8 Servings*

¼ cup brown sugar
1 tablespoon chili powder
1 teaspoon cumin
1 teaspoon cinnamon
1 teaspoon salt
¼ teaspoon pepper
⅛ teaspoon ground hot red pepper

} *Combine.*

1 pork shoulder, pork butt (4 to 5 pounds)
or pork loin rib end

} *Rub spice mixture all over pork.
Place on top of onions.*

½ cup ketchup
2 tablespoons Dijon or brown spicy mustard
1 cup chicken broth or water

} *Add to slow cooker.*

*Cover and set to 6 to 8 hours of cook time,
until pork is very tender and pulls away
effortlessly. Let cool. Pull apart pork
into shreds.*

1 cup favorite prepared BBQ sauce
⅓ juices from slow cooker

} *Mix together with shredded pork.*

12 slider rolls or 8 small hamburger buns

} *Top and serve with
Tri-Color Cole Slaw (see page 90),
Sweet Potato Steak Fries (see page 140)
and dill pickle spears.*

TIP:
*Can be made one day ahead
and reheated with juices.*

Sweet Potato Steak Fries

Preheat oven to 450°F.

4 sweet potatoes, cut into ⅛ lengthwise
(about ¼-inch thick)

} Place on lightly greased baking sheet.

2 tablespoons coconut oil

2 to 3 sprigs fresh rosemary,
leaves removed and chopped or
1 tablespoon dried

} Toss together with hands to coat well.
Bake turning occasionally, 35 to 50 minutes,
or until golden and crisp.

Sea salt } Sprinkle before serving.

*Makes about
8 Servings*

*Steak Fries are
irresistible and this version
with sweet potatoes compliments
the spiciness of the pulled pork
just right.*

A fast, easy appetizer for your guests to have with drinks while they arrive.

Macho Nachos

1 pound ground beef } *Brown beef in skillet.*

1 envelope taco seasoning mix
¾ cup water } *Add water and seasoning mix to medium skillet. Cook, 15 minutes or until beef is done and sauce is thickened.*

2 tablespoons chipotle peppers in sauce, chopped } *Stir chipotle into beef mixture. Set aside.*

1 bag (12 to 14 ounces) tortilla chips
2 cups (8 ounces) shredded Colby Jack cheese } *Alternately layer chips and cheese, then top with ground beef mixture on large baking sheet, pizza pan or ovenproof platter.*

Bake, 10 minutes or until cheese melts and heated through.

1 tomato, chopped
1 cup shredded lettuce
1 cup sour cream
1 cup prepared guacamole (See page 77)
½ cup sliced black pitted olives
2 jalapeños, fresh or pickled, sliced (optional) } *Top with remaining ingredients.*

Makes about 8 Servings

Savory Spicy Salsa

2 cups cherry or teardrop tomatoes

1 onion, quartered

2 garlic cloves, peeled

1 green pepper, sliced

1 red pepper, sliced

2 tablespoons extra virgin olive oil

2 tablespoons canned chipotle peppers with sauce

1 jalapeño, seeded and halved with stem removed (optional)

1 teaspoon ground cumin

Preheat oven to 425° F.

Combine on shallow baking pan. Bake, stirring occasionally, 30 minutes or until soft and caramelized. Let cool. Blend in food processor until almost smooth.

1 lime, zested and juiced

1 small bunch cilantro, chopped (about 1 cup)

Salt and pepper

Add lime and cilantro. Serve.

Makes about 1½ Cups

TIPS:

Serve with assorted tortilla chips. Can be made one day ahead.

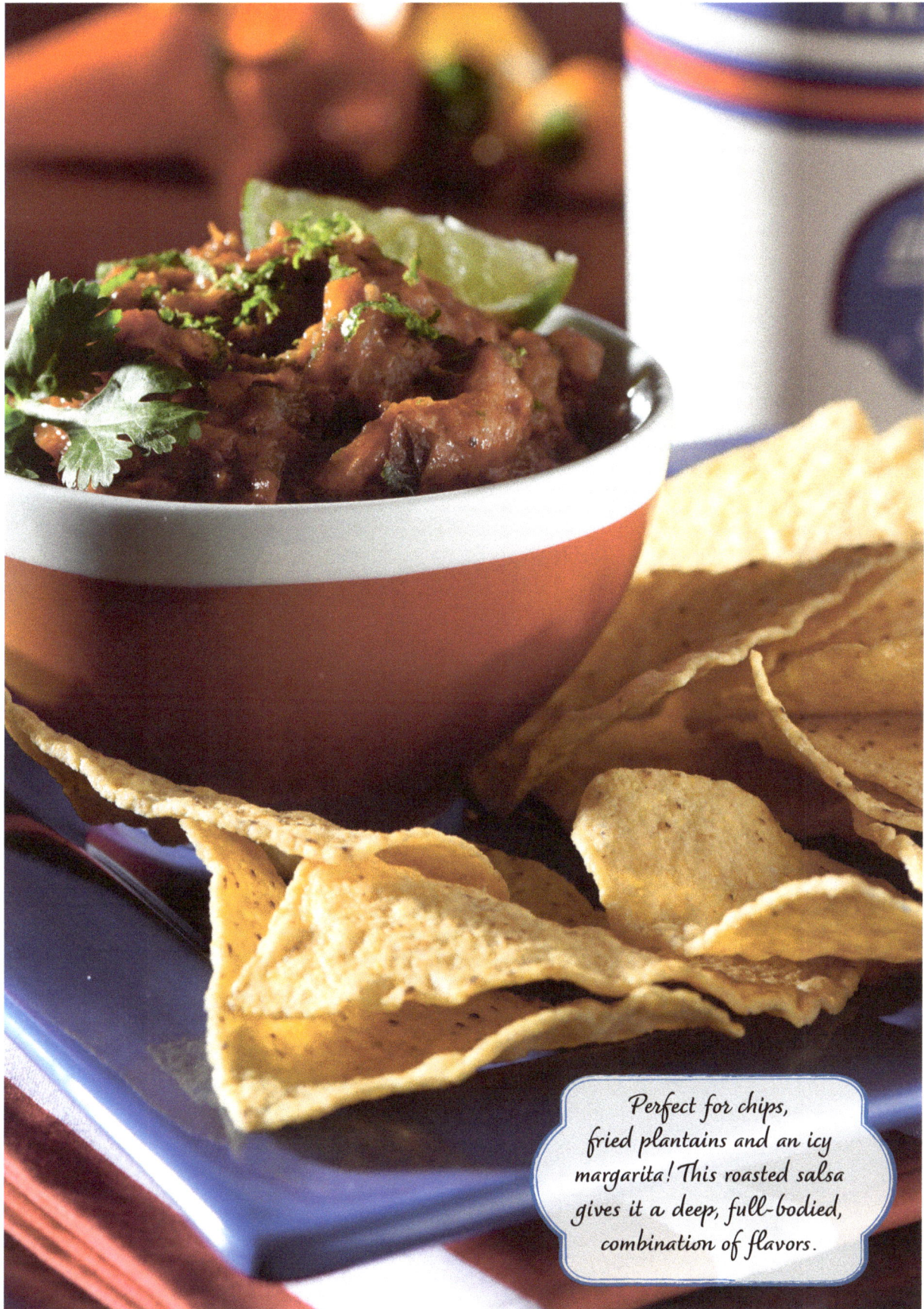

Perfect for chips, fried plantains and an icy margarita! This roasted salsa gives it a deep, full-bodied, combination of flavors.

Mango Salsa *with* Cinnamon Sugared Pita Chips

2 mangoes, peeled and coarsely chopped
1 red pepper, chopped
1 small red onion, chopped
1 bunch cilantro, chopped (about 1 cup)
2 limes, zested and juiced
Salt and pepper

} Combine in large bowl.

Chill.

Makes about 2 Cups

TIP:

Can be made one day ahead.

Cinnamon Sugared Pita Chips

Preheat oven to 425ºF.

1 package (8 ounces) 4 whole wheat or regular pitas, each cut into 8 wedges

} *Place in single layer on parchment-lined baking sheet.*

2 tablespoons butter, melted

} *Brush on pita wedges.*

1 tablespoon sugar
1 teaspoon cinnamon

} *Combine and sprinkle evenly on pita wedges.*

Bake, 6 to 7 minutes, or until lightly browned.

Makes 32 Pita Chips

TIP:

Can be made three days ahead.

This colorful salsa is great for chips and is also a wonderful topper on fish tacos, grilled chicken and hamburgers.

This recipe is one of my children's favorites and was made at my home as a child. It was served at every party when they were growing up and brought to many friends houses. This is our version with some wonderful filling suggestions.

Stromboli

1 pound prepared pizza dough (see page 42)
1 tablespoon extra virgin olive oil

} *Line 12½ x 17½ x 1-inch half sheet pan or rimmed baking sheet with parchment paper, drizzle with olive oil. Gently press pizza dough into 15 x 11-inch rectangle in prepared pan. Let rest, uncovered 30 minutes.*

Makes 12 Slices

Prepare one of the following filling selections:

Pepperoni/Mozzarella

2 tablespoons grated Parmesan cheese
1½ cups shredded mozzarella
1 bag (6 to 8 ounces) sliced pepperoni

} *Sprinkle dough with Parmesan cheese. Top with mozzarella and pepperoni in single layer.*

Spinach/Mozzarella

2 tablespoons grated Parmesan cheese
2 cups shredded mozzarella cheese
1 pound fresh spinach, cooked and squeezed dry
salt and pepper

} *Sprinkle dough with Parmesan cheese. Top with mozzarella and cooked spinach.*

Eggplant/ Mozzarella

2 tablespoons grated Parmesan cheese
2 cups shredded mozzarella
½ cup Fresh Marinara Sauce (see page 167)
6 lengthwise slices breaded or grilled eggplant

} *Sprinkle dough with Parmesan cheese. Top with mozzarella. Spread with sauce. Top with single layer of cooked eggplant.*

To Assemble Stromboli:

Preheat oven to 375°F. Line rimmed baking sheet with parchment paper.
EGG WASH (mix 1 egg yolk beaten with 1 teaspoon water). Brush outer edges of dough with Egg Wash.
Rolling gently starting on long side, roll prepared dough towards yourself, tucking ends as you roll.
Place seam-side down on prepared baking sheet.
Brush with remaining Egg Wash and sprinkle with additional Parmesan cheese.
Bake, 25 to 30 minutes or until golden. Let cool and slice on a diagonal into 1-inch slices.
Serve, if desired, with heated marinara sauce for great dipping.

TIPS: *Can be made and frozen after baked up to three months ahead.*
To reheat, wrap in foil and bake at 350°F, 25 minutes or until heated through.

Can substitute with frozen pizza dough or buy from your local pizzeria.

Meatball Parmesan Subs

Preheat oven to 400°F.

6 long, Italian rolls (about 8 inches) } Slice in half lengthwise and place on heavy-duty aluminum sheets big enough to wrap.

12 Italian Meatballs (see page 115), heated and sliced in half } Divide evenly among rolls.

1 ball (8 ounces) fresh or store bought mozzarella

1 cup Fresh Marinara (see page 167) or Italian 'Gravy' (see page 113)

¼ cup grated Parmesan cheese } Divide evenly to top meatballs.

Wrap with foil and heat in oven, 15 minutes or until cheese is melted and meatballs are heated through.

Keep in insulated container until halftime or serve immediately.

Makes 6 Subs

TIP:

Fresh mozzarella is best, but store brand can be used as well.

The secret to a good meatball sub is the meatballs and the rolls. Use my Italian Meatball recipe and a generous amount of mozzarella cheese for a mouthwatering treat. We would bring these to eat at halftime for Giants football home games. We used our leftover Sunday gravy meatballs for a fantastic game day treat!

Grandma's Pizza

Pizza Sauce:

2 large cloves garlic, chopped
2 tablespoons olive oil
} Cook over low heat in medium saucepan and simmer until fragrant, about 1 minute.

Makes about 3½ cups

1 can (32 ounces) Italian-style plum tomatoes, pureed in blender
1 teaspoon dried oregano
Salt and pepper
} Add and cook over medium heat, about 20 minutes. Let cool.

Pizza Assembly:

Preheat oven to 400°F.

1 pound fresh pizza dough* (See page 42)
2 tablespoons extra virgin olive oil
1 tablespoon cornmeal
} Brush olive oil in 12½ x 17½ x 1-inch half sheet pan or 14-inch pizza pan.

Sprinkle with cornmeal. This gives the pizza a rustic brick oven look and feel.

Makes about 12 servings

Press pizza dough to the edges of prepared pan. Let rest uncovered 30 minutes.

Bake 8 to 10 minutes or until lightly browned. (At this point, pizza can be wrapped and frozen up to 3 weeks).

6 to 8 ounces mozzarella, thinly sliced
1 cup prepared Pizza Sauce (use remaining for a second pizza or freeze for later use.)
} Raise oven temperature to 425°F.

Top evenly with slices.
Spoon on prepared pizza sauce evenly.

¼ cup grated Parmesan cheese
} Sprinkle over pizza.

Bake on bottom oven rack for 10 minutes. Move to the top rack for 5 to 10 minutes or until bottom is crispy and top is golden.

TIPS:
*Can also use defrosted, store-bought frozen pizza dough or purchase from local pizzeria.
Can be baked on pizza stone for extra crispy crust.
Let it rest 5 minutes before cutting. Kitchen shears work best.
Cut them into squares or wedges. Also delicious served at room temperature.
Pizza Sauce and assembled pizza can be made ahead and frozen. Do not defrost frozen pizza.
Bake at 425°F as above.

My mother-in-law was a terrific cook. She was famous for her Friday night homemade pizza. She had rectangular baking pans that were perfectly seasoned from overuse, giving the pizza its wonderfully crispy crust.

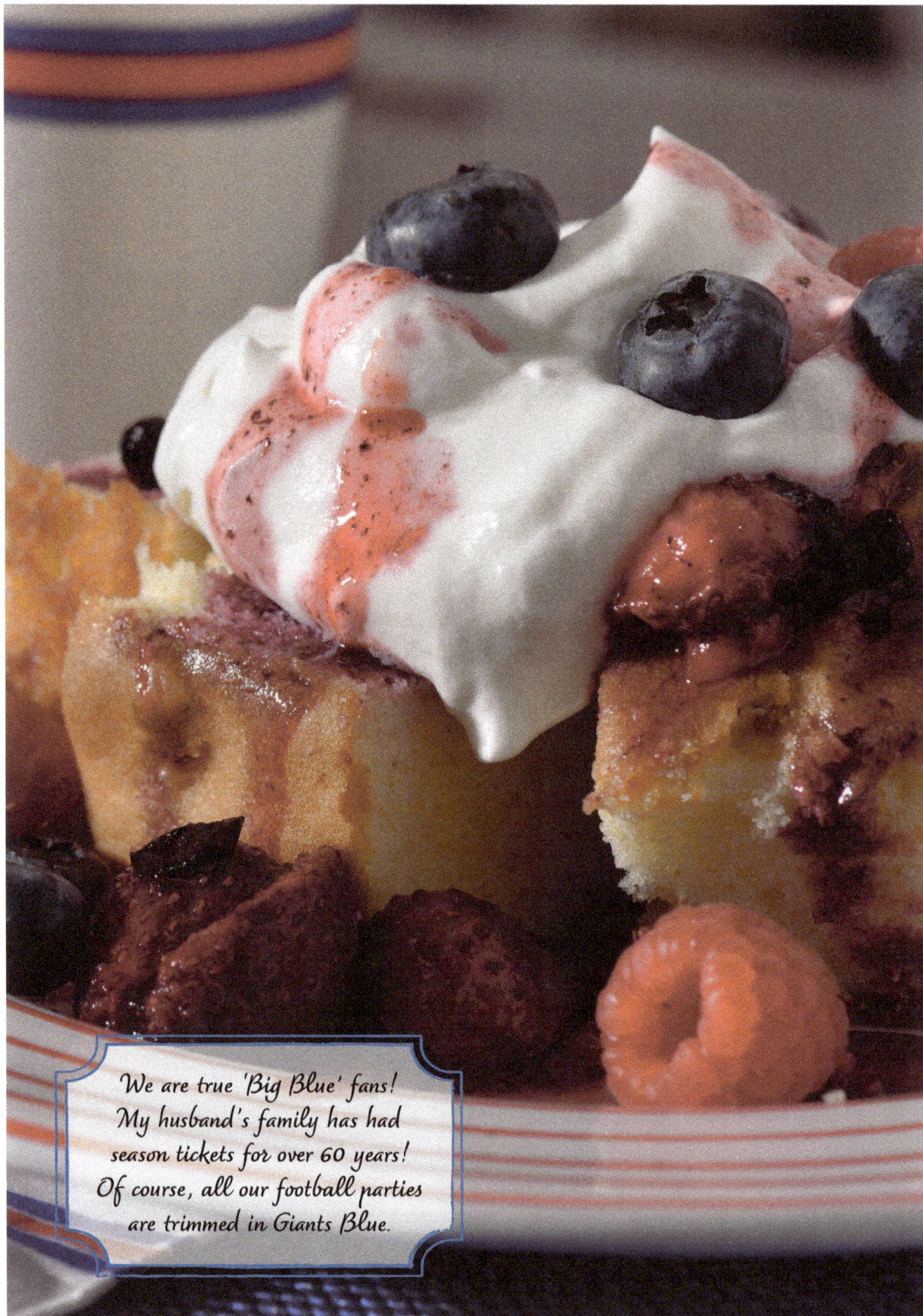

We are true 'Big Blue' fans!
My husband's family has had
season tickets for over 60 years!
Of course, all our football parties
are trimmed in Giants Blue.

'Big Blue' Berry Lemon Zested Pound Cake

Preheat oven to 325°F.

Spray 10-inch bundt pan with non-stick cooking spray.
Dust with flour, tapping to remove excess flour.

3 cups cake flour*

1½ teaspoons baking powder

1 teaspoon salt

Combine in bowl.

2 cups (4 sticks) butter, softened

1 box (1 pound) confectioner's sugar

Combine in bowl of electric mixer. Beat on low speed until combined, then beat on high speed, 3 minutes or until light and fluffy.

6 eggs

2 teaspoons vanilla extract

1 lemon, zested

Combine in medium bowl. Add slowly to butter mixture and beat on low speed until blended.

1 cup heavy cream**

Pour alternately with flour mixture and beat on low speed until blended.

Bake, 1 to 1½ hours, until a toothpick inserted in center of cake comes out clean.

Let cool, 15 minutes, and revert on wire rack.

Completely cool.

Garnish with dusting of confectioner's sugar.

Berry topping

2 cups blueberries

1 cup raspberries

1 cup sliced strawberries

¼ cup sugar

1 lemon, zested and juiced

Toss together. Serve with pound cake.

TIPS:

*Substitute with all-purpose flour if desired. Cake flour makes it extra light.

** Can substitute with whole milk. Can be frozen up to 1 month.

Great Memorial Day or Fourth of July dessert, too!

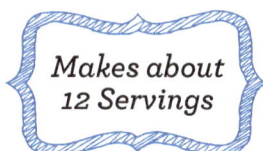

Makes about 12 Servings

155

I made over 50 cheesecakes to taste test when I entered a NY Lindy's cheesecake contest at age 16. My father was my happy taste tester! This recipe won and I hope it's a winner in your home as well.

New York-Style Cheesecake

Preheat oven to 325°F.

Place shallow baking pan on lower rack in oven (half sheet pan works perfectly) and fill with at least 1 inch water. The moisture from the steam helps prevent the cheesecake from cracking.

Open springform pan. Insert the bottom pan upside down and close springform pan.
Line 9-inch springform pan* with circle of parchment paper.
This method allows your cheesecake to slide right off onto your serving plate much easier.
Wrap outside of springform with heavy-duty aluminum foil to prevent
any seeping of butter through pan when baking.

Makes about 16 Servings

Crust:

1½ cups graham cracker crumbs
2 tablespoons sugar
¼ cup (½ stick) butter, melted

Combine in small bowl and firmly press into bottom of prepared springform pan.

Bake, 8 minutes. Cool.

Batter:

5 packages (8 ounces each) softened cream cheese
1¾ cups sugar

Combine in large bowl of electric mixer. Beat on high speed until light and fluffy, about 5 minutes.

6 eggs

Add eggs one at a time and beat on low speed just until smooth, about 1 to 2 minutes. DO NOT OVERBEAT. This also helps prevent cheesecake from cracking.

½ cup heavy cream
1 teaspoon vanilla extract
3 tablespoons all-purpose flour

Add and beat on low speed until smooth, about 1 minute. Pour batter into prepared pan. Place on middle rack of oven.

Bake 1 hour and 30 minutes or until center is almost set.

Let cool.

Chill 2 hours or overnight.

TIPS:

Serve, if desired, with fresh strawberries.

* Can use 10-inch spring form pan and bake 1 hour and 20 minutes.

graduation

Graduation Party

Eggplant Caponata

Hummus

Multi-Color Olive Tapenade

Classic Eggplant Parmesan

Fresh Marinara Sauce

Fabulous Fresh Pesto

Tri-Color Sausage and Peppers

New Potato Salad *with* Dill

Grilled Zucchini and Yellow Squash *with* Fresh Mint

Fresh Tomato Basil Salad *with* Ricotta Salata

Fresh Fruit Salad *with* Tri-Color Citrus Dressing

Love Knots

Lemon Curd Cheesecake

Eggplant Caponata

1 large eggplant

1 sweet onion, coarsely chopped

3 cloves garlic, finely chopped

2 cups cherry or grape tomatoes, cut in half

2 tablespoons extra virgin olive oil

Preheat oven to 350°F.

Add onto lightly greased baking pan.

Bake, 30 minutes or until eggplant is soft when pierced with fork.

Let cool.

Remove eggplant skin (it will peel off very easily and will be very soft).
Chop eggplant into small pieces.

½ cup pitted Niçoise olives, chopped

1 bunch Italian parsley, stems removed, chopped (about 1 cup)

Salt and pepper

Combine with eggplant and cooked vegetables in large bowl.

Mix well.
Serve immediately or chill until serving time.

TIPS:

Can bake eggplant one day ahead.
Can assemble recipe one day ahead.

Serve with chips or toasted pita bread for an instant party!

Each Recipe Makes 2 Cups

Hummus

2 cans (16 ounces each) chickpeas, drained

2 cloves garlic, peeled

2 lemons, zested

2 tablespoons extra virgin olive oil

2 tablespoons tahini paste

salt and pepper

Combine all ingredients in food processor until smooth.

Serve with toasted pita chips*.

TIP:

*To make your own pita chips, cut pita bread into eighths with a knife or kitchen shears. Drizzle with olive oil and sprinkle with sea salt. Bake at 400°F, about 5 minutes or until toasted.

I usually serve my Eggplant Caponata with my Hummus because they complement each other beautifully.

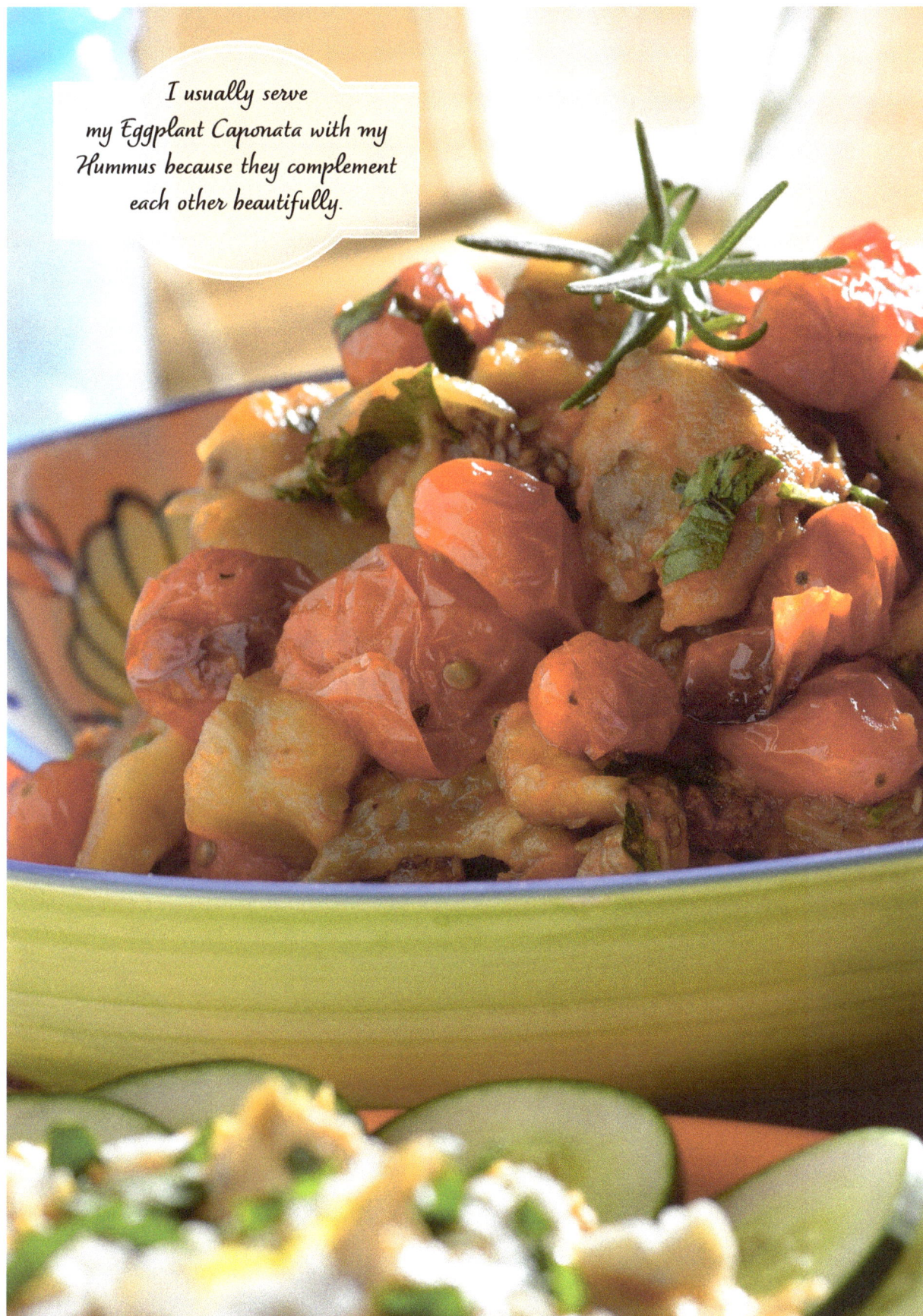

Multi-Color Olive Tapenade

1 bunch Italian parsley, stems removed

2 cloves garlic, peeled

} *Combine and process until finely chopped in food processor.*

1 can (6 ounces) pitted black olives, drained

1 can (6 ounces) pitted green Castelvetrano olives (my favorite), drained

1 small red pepper, seeded and quartered

} *Add to food processor and pulse until coarsely chopped. Spoon into large bowl.*

2 tablespoons capers

¼ cup extra virgin olive oil

2 tablespoons white balsamic vinegar

Salt and pepper

} *Add to olive mixture and stir until combined.*

Serve immediately or chill until ready to serve. Serve with assorted crackers and sliced, toasted baguettes.

Makes about 2 Cups

TIPS:

Can be made one day ahead and chilled.

Great with a slice of velvety stinky cheese like Gorgonzola or a rich Camembert.

An impressive appetizer as a quick, last minute choice for unexpected company.

My oldest daughter Maria says, "Whether it's as little as a high school musical afterparty or as big as a college graduation from NYU, my mom always makes this when my parents are proud of Marisa or myself. This reminds me of a celebratory reason to get together with family and friends, as it's always somewhere in the middle of our table."

Classic Eggplant Parmesan

Makes about 10-12 Servings

1½ cups all-purpose flour
1 teaspoon salt
¼ teaspoon pepper

Combine in shallow bowl or plate.

4 eggs, beaten
2 tablespoons grated Parmesan cheese
2 tablespoons water

Combine in shallow bowl or plate.

Enough canola oil to fill skillet ¼-inch deep and one swirl of extra virgin olive oil

Heat on medium high heat in large deep skillet (Oil is ready if it bubbles when dropping a little egg batter into it.)

2 medium eggplant (or one large), peeled and thinly sliced into ⅛-inch thick, crosswise rounds

Dip one eggplant slice at a time: first in flour mixture, then egg mixture.

Place immediately in oil and cook, about 2 to 3 minutes per side, or until lightly browned.

Drain on layers of paper towel to absorb any excess oil. Repeat frying with remaining slices.

2½ cups Fresh Marinara sauce (see page 167)
1 pound mozzarella, thinly sliced
¼ cup grated Parmesan cheese
¼ cup grated Pecorino Romano cheese

Spread ½ cup sauce in 13 x 9-inch casserole.

Top with one-third prepared eggplant slices, one-third remaining sauce, half mozzarella, and one-third grated cheeses.

TIPS:

The fried eggplant can be layered with parchment and frozen up to one month ahead.

The entire recipe can be made ahead and chilled for two days or frozen up to one month.

Just make plenty extra for delicious leftover sandwiches!

Repeat layers, ending with third layer of eggplant slices.

Top with remaining sauce and remaining Parmesan and Romano cheeses.

Bake covered with aluminum foil, 30 minutes.

Remove, cover and bake additional 5 minutes, or until browned and bubbly.

Let sit at least 15 minutes before serving.

Fresh Marinara Sauce

8 cloves garlic, chopped

¼ cup extra virgin olive oil

} *Cook on low heat in large skillet, 5 minutes or until soft but not browned.*

2 cans (28 ounces each) San Marzano plum tomatoes, undrained

} *Add and blend with immersion blender right in skillet until smooth (or puree in blender before adding to skillet).*

10 basil leaves, rolled and sliced thin into ribbons (NOTE: This is called chiffonade)

Salt and pepper

} *Add and cook, 30 minutes or until bubbly.*

Makes about 8 Cups

TIP:

Recipe can be halved but I suggest making this big batch and freezing it in small containers for convenience.

The secret to the ideal marinara — a sweeter and stronger tomato with less seeds. My parents always used San Marzano tomatoes growing up as classic, Italian traditions play a major mantle in my cooking.

Fabulous Fresh Pesto

2 cloves garlic

1 large bunch Italian parsley, stems removed (about 1 cup)

1 large bunch fresh basil leaves, stems removed (about 2 cups)*

} *Add to food processor. Process until smooth.*

½ cup extra virgin olive oil

¼ cup pignoli nuts**

¼ cup grated Parmesan cheese

¼ cup grated Pecorino Romano cheese

Squeeze of a lemon (about 1 tablespoon)

Salt and pepper

} *Drizzle olive oil slowly into running food processor. Add remaining ingredients.*

TIPS:

*If you want to keep pesto extra green try blanching the basil. To blanch basil, dip basil leaves in boiling water, 2 to 5 seconds. Immediately plunge in ice water bath. Remove and pat dry.

**Can substitute with walnuts or almonds.

Toss on your favorite pasta. Also great on fish and poultry.

Freezes fabulously! Make small containers or fill ice cube trays to have small amounts handy for everyday cooking, too.

We grow tons of basil in our garden in the summer. It's my ultimate herb!

My favorite flavor combination is basil and garlic. My husband and I love our garden in the summer. He is in charge of the tomatoes and vegetables and I am in charge of the herbs. I plant extra basil for pesto all summer long.

Makes about 1½ Cups

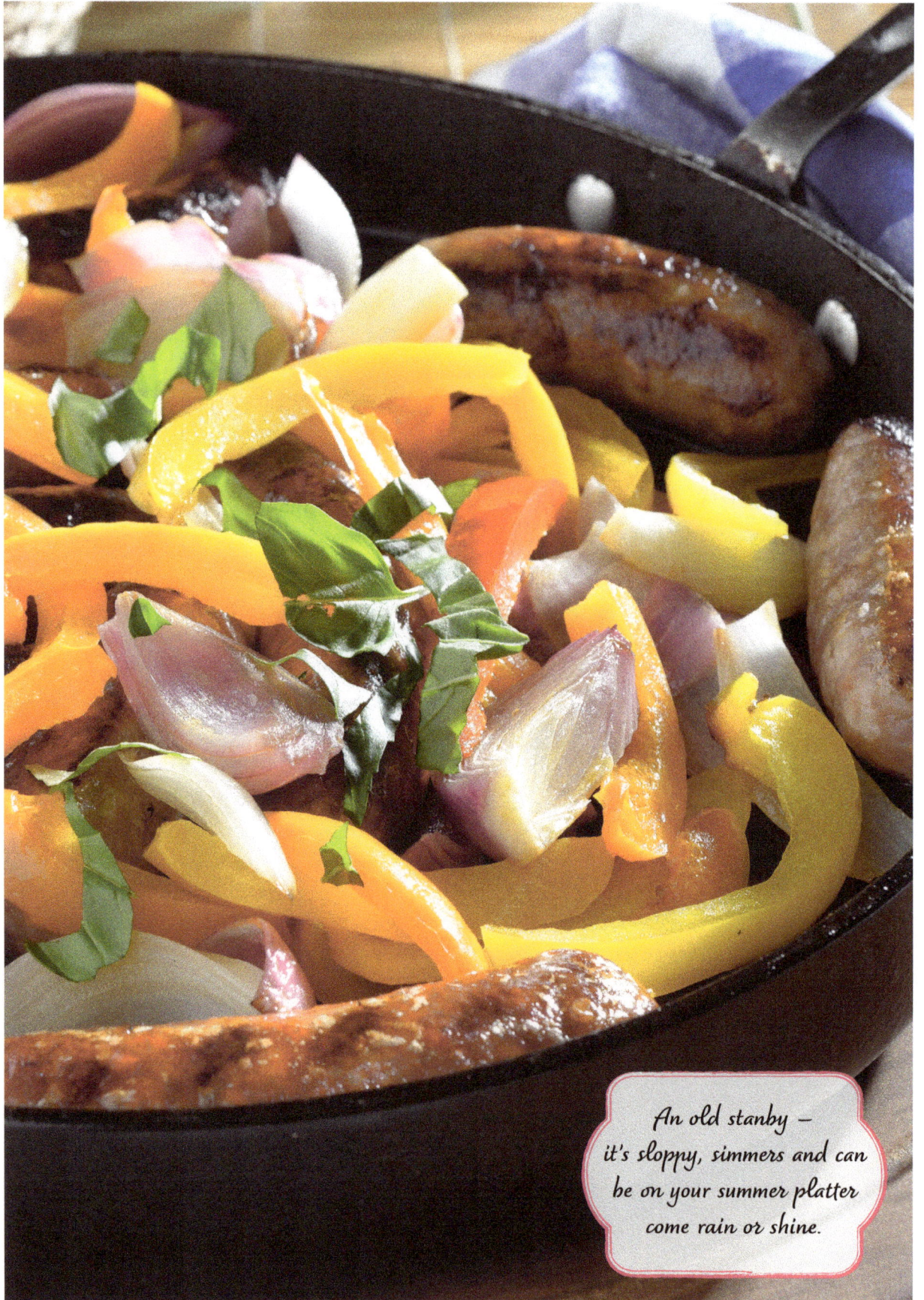

An old stanby —
it's sloppy, simmers and can
be on your summer platter
come rain or shine.

Tri-Color Sausage and Peppers

2 pounds Italian link sausages

} *Brown over medium high heat in large cast iron skillet, or grill pan, until almost done.*

Remove and slice into 1-inch diagonal slices.

2 tablespoons extra virgin olive oil

1 large Vidalia or red onion, sliced

3 medium red, green, orange or yellow peppers, seeded and sliced

} *Add to same skillet and cook over medium high heat until begins to soften.*

Add sausage and cook, 10 minutes, stirring constantly, until browned and cooked through.

¼ cup dry white wine

} *Add white wine and let evaporate (deglaze).*

1 cup fresh basil leaves, thinly sliced

} *Garnish with basil leaves.*

Serve hot.

Makes 8 Servings

TIP:

Serve as an entree by itself or with Italian rolls for the perfect sausage and pepper sandwiches.

New Potato Salad *with* Dill

1 cup mayonnaise

¼ cup sour cream or plain Greek yogurt

¼ cup whole grain mustard

1 bunch dill, coarsely chopped

2 tablespoons extra virgin olive oil

3 tablespoons white wine or
white balsamic vinegar

Salt and pepper

Combine is large bowl and stir until blended.

2 pounds red bliss potatoes,
sliced into quarters

1 teaspoon salt

In a large sauce pan, boil 10 minutes or until tender.

Drain and let cool, 5 minutes.

Combine with mayonnaise mixture. Chill until ready to serve.

Makes about 8-10 Servings

TIP:

Garnish with extra dill sprigs and red onion rings.

Looks gorgeous with your summer buffet!

Grilled Zucchini and Yellow Squash
with Fresh Mint

2 cloves garlic, finely chopped

¼ cup extra virgin olive oil

Salt and pepper

} *Combine in 2-cup heatproof glass measuring cup. Microwave for 1 minute (or heat mixture in small saucepan over low heat, 3 minutes). This will make garlic sweeter, removing bitterness and infusing olive oil with flavor. I make a big batch of this mixture and use it for most of my antipasti preparation. This mixture can stay in the refrigerator up to one week.*

2 zucchini, thinly sliced lengthwise

2 yellow squash, thinly sliced lengthwise

} *Brush with olive oil mixture.*

Grill or broil until done.

1 cup fresh mint leaves, torn

} *Top and serve.*

Makes about 8 Servings

TIPS:

Serve at room temperature.

Delicious with crumbled feta, too!

Just a simple side to accompany any occasion.

Fresh Tomato Basil Salad *with* Ricotta Salata

¼ cup extra virgin olive oil

3 garlic cloves, chopped

Combine in 2-cup heatproof glass measuring cup. Microwave for 1 minute (or heat mixture in small saucepan over low heat, 3 minutes). This will make garlic sweeter, removing bitterness and infusing olive oil with flavor. I make a big batch of this mixture and use it for most of my anti-pasti preparation. This mixture can stay in the refrigerator up to one week.

2 tablespoons white balsamic vinegar

Add to olive oil mixture.

2 cups cherry tomatoes (red and/or yellow), halved

1 small red onion, sliced

Combine in medium bowl. Toss with olive oil mixture.

1 cup loosely packed fresh basil leaves, rolled and sliced thin into ribbons (NOTE: This is called chiffonade)

8 ounces ricotta salata, shredded

Salt and pepper

Add to tomato mixture. Garnish with additional shredded ricotta salada and basil leaves.

Makes about 2 Cups

TIPS:

This can be served over chicken cutlets for Milanese or grilled fish, or toasted bread slices for traditional bruschetta.

Recipe can be easily doubled.

Bold garden flavors are instantly refreshing when combined with the natural softness and subtle bite of the ricotta salata.

Fresh Fruit Salad *with* Tri-Color Citrus Dressing

1 orange, zested and juiced

1 lime, zested and juiced

1 lemon, zested and juiced

2 tablespoons sugar

Combine in small bowl and stir until blended. Set aside.

2 cups watermelon, scooped with melon baller or cut into small chunks

1 cup cantaloupe, scooped with melon baller or cut into small chunks

1 cup honeydew, scooped with melon baller or cut into small chunks

2 cups strawberries, halved

1 cup blueberries

Combine in large bowl.

1 cup raspberries

Toss prepared fruit with citrus dressing and top with raspberries before serving.

Garnish, if desired, with fresh mint leaves.

Makes about 16 Servings

TIPS:

Serve this salad in a watermelon boat for a clever presentation. You can even carve the name of the guest of honor or the occasion in the watermelon for a personal touch. This will definitely give it a WOW factor!

Can make dressing one day ahead and chill.

Cut fruit one day ahead and store individually in plastic food store bags in refrigerator.

It's pretty to look at and the citrus dressing brings all the fruit flavors together.

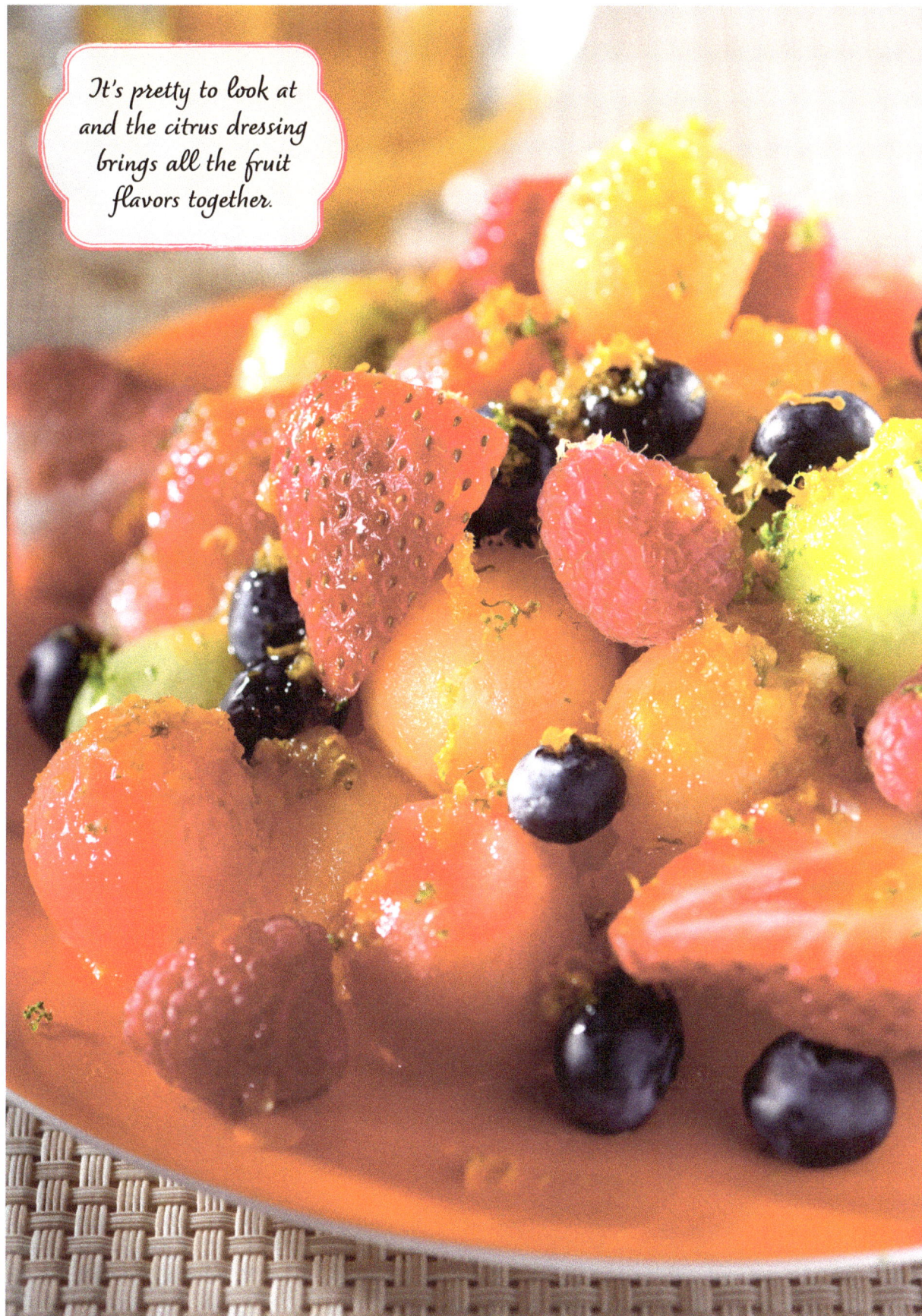

Love Knots Cookies:

Preheat oven to 325°F.
Line baking sheets with parchment paper.

4 cups unbleached all-purpose flour

1 tablespoon baking powder

1 teaspoon baking soda

1 teaspoon salt

Combine in medium bowl. Set aside.

1 cup (2 sticks) butter, softened

1½ cups sugar

Add to large bowl of electric mixer. Beat on high speed until light and creamy, about 5 minutes.

1 container (15 ounces) whole milk ricotta (about 1¾ cups)

Add and beat on medium high speed, about 2 minutes or until smooth.

2 eggs

2 teaspoons anise or lemon extract*

1 teaspoon vanilla extract

Add and beat on low speed, about 1 minute or until blended.

Slowly add flour mixture on low speed until combined and then beat on high speed, 30 seconds. Use a 1½-inch ice cream scoop or drop heaping tablespoons on prepared baking sheets 2-inches apart.
ROLL gently into smooth balls.

Bake, 9 to 11 minutes or until puffed.

DO NOT OVERBAKE. Cookie should be light brown on bottom side and light on top. Soft when touched and springs back slightly.

Let cool on wire rack and then coat with icing.

TIPS:

*I usually use anise flavor for Christmas and lemon flavor for springtime and special occasions.

Use small 1½-inch ice cream scooper to make evenly sized cookies.

It's great to have a partner, one person ice and one person sprinkle!

If icing gets too thick add a few drops of half and half at a time to make thinner.

Cookie dough can be prepare ahead, chilled for up to four hours, and rolled into balls for smoother cookies. Dough can also be frozen up to one month ahead.

These cookies freeze beautifully, unfrosted, up to two months. Best to ice day of serving.

Makes about 60 Cookies

These Italian cookies were traditionally made at weddings because they were a combination of a sweet bread dough tied into a knot. I first learned to make them from my neighbor growing up, the lovely Mrs. Fontana, but they were yeast based. My family simplified them with baking powder, and my in-laws also had a version using baking powder and cream cheese. After many trials and tests, I discovered ricotta makes them a little softer and received my daughters' and friends' best votes! I alter the flavor and sprinkles for the seasons. We traditionally use multicolored nonpareils, but change the colored sprinkles based on the event at hand.

Love Knots Icing:

¼ cup half and half or light cream	*Microwave in heatproof glass measuring cup, 20 seconds.*
2 teaspoons anise extract or 1 teaspoon lemon extract mixed with 1 teaspoon fresh lemon juice* 2 to 2¼ cups confectioner's sugar	*Slowly add and stir with small wire whisk until blended and thick but still spreadable. Keep covered with plastic wrap while working so icing does not harden.*
Assorted sprinkles, colored nonpareils, or use any desired color for your occasion	*Spoon icing on cookies one by one and immediately top with sprinkles before icing hardens.*

Lemon Curd Cheesecake

Preheat oven to 350°F.

Place shallow baking pan on lower rack in oven (half sheet pan works perfectly) and fill with at least 1 inch water. The moisture from the steam helps prevent the cheesecake from cracking.

Open springform pan. Insert the bottom pan upside down and close springform pan.
Line 9-inch springform pan* with circle of parchment paper.
This method allows your cheesecake to slide right off onto your serving plate much easier.
Wrap outside of springform with heavy-duty aluminum foil to prevent
any seeping of butter through pan when baking.

Crust:

1 ½ cups graham cracker crumbs
2 tablespoons sugar
¼ cup (½ stick) butter, melted

} *Combine in small bowl and firmly press into bottom of springform pan.*

Bake, 8 minutes. Cool.

Batter:

4 packages (8 ounces each) cream cheese, softened
1 ½ cups sugar

} *Combine in large bowl of electric mixer. Beat on high speed until light and fluffy, about 5 minutes.*

5 eggs

} *Add eggs one at a time and beat on low speed just until smooth, about 1 to 2 minutes. DO NOT OVERBEAT. This also helps prevent cheesecake from cracking.*

1 pint (16 ounces) sour cream
1 teaspoon vanilla extract
2 tablespoons all-purpose flour
1 lemon, zested

} *Add and beat on low speed until blended, about 1 minute. Pour batter into prepared pan. Place on middle rack of oven. Bake 1 hour and 15 minutes or until center is almost set.*

Let cool.

Chill 2 hours or overnight. Top with Lemon Curd (see page 34) and garnish with additional lemon zest.

TIPS:

Can be made and frozen up to one month ahead.
Can make lemon curd one week ahead.
Can substitute Lemon Curd with store bought or jarred lemon curd.
Garnish with lemon slices and fresh mint.

Makes 16 Servings

HOW TO USE THIS BOOK

Recipe Book Structure

From my experience styling thousands of recipes, I wanted to create a recipe book that was easier to read. When I have to prepare a multitude of recipes at one time, I rewrite the recipes so I can prepare them quickly and more efficiently. This practice gave me the idea that I am now demonstrating in this book. Here, you see the ingredients needed and the method at the same time. I used brackets to list the ingredients on the left and placed the method directly to the right. In this arrangement, you can anticipate what you need for each step of the recipe easily, know exactly what measurements you need, and therefore avoid mistakes. It also helps me with my grocery and preparation lists.

Ingredients and Terms Used

Extra Virgin Olive Oil: This is a family favorite and the most essential ingredient in my kitchen. It has always been a staple since I was a child. It's one of the healthiest oils to cook with but should not be used with high heat, as this will alter its structure and flavor. Use butter, canola or peanut oil for high heat instead.

Flour: Use all-purpose flour.

Eggs: Use large eggs.

Butter: Always use unsalted, especially in baking.

Salt and pepper: I list them often in recipes. Seasoning is important in making all of your cooking hard effort come together. Use amounts to your liking. I usually season at the end of cooking unless specified when used in a coating or baking.

Sauté: In cooking school, I learned the saying, "hot pan, cold oil." This means always heat your pan first and then add your oil, butter, etc., to the pan before cooking. This helps prevent your meat or food items from sticking, and also makes a beautiful seared or browned edge on your meat items to seal in the juices. Heat your pan a few minutes on medium high heat, then add your oil for about one more minute. Then, begin cooking to your liking or according to the recipe.

BPB: A baking term I learned in pastry class in culinary school. For all of your cake pans, baking pans, etc., spray your pan with non-stick cooking spray or rub with butter, line with baking parchment paper, then spray or butter again. (Thus the term BPB.) Your baked items will never stick again. It's a foolproof way to remove them without the disaster of ruining your hard work.

Red or White Wine Vinegar, Red or White Balsamic Vinegar: I use these quite often because they have a fresh look and still give your salad a nice, rich balanced flavor. Of course, substitute with any of your favorite wine-based vinegars.

Flavored Vinegars and Oils: Experiment by substituting any flavor you desire to make a whole new flavoring for a dressing and/or dish. I personally use fig, raspberry, sherry and herb infused vinegars often.

Citrus Zest: I love citrus flavors in salads and incorporate lemons, limes and oranges by using the zest of the skin and the juice.

Parmesan Cheese: I recommend using only Parmigiano Reggiano. It's so buttery and nutty, and will make so many dishes sing.

Pecorino Romano Cheese: This cheese is a little saltier than Parmesan and gives a nice bite and creaminess to many of my recipes. I actually often use Parmesan and Pecorino Romano together to give some of my Italian-based recipes a perfect blend of tanginess, saltiness and nuttiness.

My Favorite Tools

Good Set of Professional Knives: I cannot stress enough how important it is to have a set of good professional knives. A good set of sharp knives enables you to work more efficiently in the kitchen and is much safer than an inexpensive set. You can buy one knife at a time and start to build a personal set for your needs. I would suggest a good quality chef knife to start, utility knife for multitasking jobs, a paring knife for small items, and a long serrated knife for bread and cake slicing.

Zester/Narrow Zester with Handle: It's long and usually has a handle. It's perfect for zesting citrus in a flash and can also be used for grating garlic, chocolate or hard cheeses, too.

Metal Scraper: I keep this tool on my cutting board during all my prep. It has a thin metal base, about six inches long and four inches wide, with a wooden handle on one end. It's terrific when scraping flour off your board after baking and makes clean up a breeze. Also, it's handy when scooping up any chopped small veggies or herbs to go right into the skillet during cooking.

Offset Spatula: A must in your kitchen so maybe buy a few. It's a small metal spatula that bends by the handle. Makes easy spreading and frosting on cakes and desserts.

Immersion Blender: This no hassle device saves time and cleanup. It's great when blending canned tomatoes for sauces and sautéed veggies for making soup right in the pan or pot you're cooking in.

Small and Large Food Processor: I use my small food processor often, especially when I need to chop a good amount of garlic, onion, parsley or herbs for entertaining. It's also great for making quick, fresh bread crumbs. A large food processor makes cookie crumbs as well as pastry and pizza doughs in a flash.

Large Standing Mixer: Just a joy for mixing, baking, whipping, etc. It practically mixes by itself. You can run your mixer hands-free while preparing your next steps.

Large Piping Star Tips: These make a simple dessert into a showpiece. Pipe your whipped cream in pretty rosettes simply and easily.

Disposable Pint or Quart Size Plastic Storage Bags: Use these to drizzle chocolate, squeeze mayonnaise or mustard easily, or even pipe whipped cream. Fill with desired ingredient, snip one end and have an instant piping bag.

Kitchen Shears: So helpful when cutting all types of food items without ruining your good knives. I especially love them when cutting pizza, through chicken bones, and snipping herbs.

Aluminum Foil and Parchment Paper: I line my baking sheets often with aluminum foil when I am cooking for a party. This does not affect the cooking process. Makes clean up easy peasy! It's imperative to line your cake pans and baking sheets with parchment paper for non-stick success in baking.

186

Entertaining Tips and Party Hints

Home sweet home

Entertaining at home is a very warm and loving way to enjoy family and friends. There is just something about the warmth of your home that makes people feel very comfortable and relaxed. Whether it be just a neighbor stopping by last minute and a glass of wine turns into an impromptu plate of pasta or planning for a big family celebration, having a gathering at home makes your guests feel special.

Inspiration with zeal

I usually get most of my ideas while food shopping. Walking down the supermarket aisles or stopping by a local farmers' market inspires me with so many ideas for cooking. Always take advantage of the season and use fruits and vegetables that are at their highest peak and availability at that time locally whenever possible. You will get the best bang for your buck while buying locally and funding the local farmers, as well as feed your family with the most nutritious and organic foods available. Take advantage of food magazines and social media, and start collecting ideas of cooking and baking that you enjoy. Food likes and dislikes are very subjective and you have to be excited and love what you are making so the dish will truly shine. Much of my inspiration has come from my family and food colleagues. Talk about what you made for dinner at your work place, school or with friends. They will share what they made and you may get a new idea to try. Especially around the holidays, everyone is talking about their favorite cookie or entrée that their family loves. Many ingredients are interchangeable in my savory recipes. Baking, though, is more of a science and you must be careful not to deviate from the measurements. Get inspired everyday and create something in your own way!

Plan and anticipate. It's all in the prep!

Because I am a food stylist, most of the success of a food shoot is in the planning, prep, research and anticipation. I have learned, with years of experience, that if you're totally prepared, the shoot can be flawless and goes smoothly. Actually, sometimes it goes too smoothly, and the clients think it was an easy day, but what they did not see was all the behind the scenes prep and hard work that made that one slice of perfect pie look gorgeous. It's the same way with entertaining. If you're prepared ahead of time and anticipate the organization needed, your party will go smoothly. Also, if there is a blip or two, maybe you forgot the sour cream for the quesadillas or burnt the bruschetta toast—just skip it and no one will even notice. Just don't worry! Once the party gets started I start to relax because most of the work is all done. So, for most of the recipes I have noted which are wonderful make-aheads and include helpful prep tips.

Mise en place!

A vital french culinary term I learned in culinary school that means "Everything in its place." It's so important to get all your ingredients organized and ready to go, including pan and baking sheet prep, before you start cooking and baking. This way you cook faster and make less mistakes.

Lists, lists, lists!

Another great planning tip is to make a series of lists. I'm an avid list maker and if you ask my husband he will tell you that I'm obsessed with sticky notes! I love the bright colored ones and use them for all my daily errands and activities that need to get done. I like the old fashioned way of writing them down as this helps me remember better, especially if it's before bedtime. Yes, I keep sticky notes on my bedside table as well as on my pocketbook and in my car. You do not want to forget an important item. If you forget an important ingredient at a food shoot it can make or break a photography job.

189

"8th Grade Graduation Celebration!"
June 12, 2004

Appetizers

Baked Brie en Croute, Blue Point Oysters with French Vinaigrette or Cocktail Sauce, Grilled Chix Wings with Hot Sauce or Bleu Cheese, Assorted Dips, Cheeses & Crudité, Fresh Mozzarella Tomato & Basil

Main Course

Grilled London Broil with Balsamic & Herbs, Sausage and Peppers, Hot Dogs, Hamburgers, Skewered Jumbo Shrimp Kebabs with Pineapple, Grilled Vegetables, Uneldited Seafood with Cranberry and Oranges, Dill Potato Salad, Bow Tie Pasta Salad with Roasted Peppers, Grilled Corn Salad with Cilantro, Lime Lime, Sauerkraut, Baked Beans

Dessert

Congratulations Cannoli Cake with chocolate, pralines and fresh whipped cream
Love Italian Knots
Brownie Bars, Chocolate chip Cookie Bars
Watermelon Boat with Fruit Salad
Ice Cream Cake

...and Basil
...chetta Topped with Sweetened Ricotta with Figs, Prosciutto and Honey
...tato Pizza with Truffle Oil, Rosemary and Parmesan Reggiano
...o Encrusted Brie with Hot Pepper
...Fresh Guacamole with Plaintain Chips

Main Course

Surf &...
...ed Grilled...
...nions ar...
...inated...
...falle...
...Chop...

Wendi's Baby Shower Brunch
July 9, 2006

Appetizers

Brie En Crosta with Raspberry and Al...
Crab and Spinach Dip with Crudite

Brunch

Potato and Egg Bites with Fontina, Asp...
Broccoli and Cheddar Quiche with...
...dish French Toast Bake with Pe...
Bacon Breadstick Wraps w/ M...
Maple Cured Spiral Ham w...
Baked Salmon with Red...
...rd Salad with Orang...
...Pecans with ...
Fresh Figs, Shri...
Home Baked Rap...
Merita's Triple...
...Jackie's Famous Scones...
Assorted Bage...

Brunch with Friends
April 23, 2011

Fresh Berry Fruit Salad with Tri-citrus Dressing
Quiche with Chorizo, Red Peppers & Pepper Jack
Blueberry Lemon Scones with Strawberry Lemon Butter
Grilled Chicken & Shrimp Caes... Salad with Semolina Cr...

Superbowl...

Appetizers

...emade Guacamo...
...p with Crust...
...rudite & chips...
...man with Lem...
Sesame...
Wings

Course

...alva
Dill &...
...h Hon...

Marisas 1st Birthday
1996

"Appetizers"

Crudite with Garlic Herb Dip
Mozzarella & Tomato Salada with Garlic Crustide

"Main Course Bar-B-Que"

Chicken Roasted in Balsamic Vinegar & Her...
Baked Ziti with Tomato & Eg...
Roasted Italian Sausage...
Hot Dogs & H...
Dilled New Potato...
Antipasto Fusilli Salad...
Baked Maple Glazed Beans...
Relish Tray (String...

"Dessert"

Birthday Cake - Watermelon Boat w...
Cannoli & Chocolate...
Whipped cre...
Ice...

Maria's 4th Birthday

Appetizers

...e Dip
...ostini
...n Tortilla Chips
...ream
...uda with
...lmond...

Shrimp & Spinach Dip with Crudite
Smoked Brie with Basil & Garlic
...erbed Goat Cheese
...d Chips & Crackers

Maria's 13th Birthday!!!!!!!
April 6, 2003

Appetizers

Baked Brie en Croute with Apricots and Toasted Almonds
Hot Artichoke and Crab Dip   Onion Dip   Seafood Spread
Grilled Quesadillas with Black Bean and Corn Salsa
Assorted European Cheeses Olives and Pates   Assorted Snacks
Little Hot Dogs in a Blanket

Main Course

...and Toasted Pignoli
...with Sauteed...
Fresh Baked...
...ed Orzo with...
Salad with Wa...
Pecans with ...
...mato Po...

Poppy's 80th Bi...
April 8, 200...

Appetizers

White Potato Pizza with Rosemary
Italian Grilled Quesadillas with Olive Ta...
Roasted Peppers, Artichokes served with...
Tomato
Hot Lump Crabmeat with...
Shrimp Cocktail with Lemon...
Semolina Crum...
Grilled Tuna with Wasabi...
Filet Mignon over Toast Cuisit...
and Pecans
Fresh Mozzarella wist...

Marisa's High School Graduation
June 22, 20013
GO KNIGHTS!

Appetizers

Sonny's Eggplant Meatballs with Fresh Mo...
South-West Medley with Fresh Guacamole...
and Corn Relish with Cheese Ques...
Middle Eastern Hummus with Whole...
Pepperoni and Spinach Mushroom...
Herb and Lemon-infused Shrimp...
Fresh Mozzarella and Tomato...
Olive Tapenade with Smoked Mea...
Baked Artichoke Dip and Ass...

Entrees

Chicken Milanese with Bruschetta...
Salad with Pomegranate...
Tricolor Sausage and...
Freshly Baked Eggplant...
Grilled Hotdogs and...
Fresh Pesto Bow-t...
Dilled Red-skinned...
Grilled Corn Barley and...
Maple-cured Bacon,...
Sauerkraut with Gr...

Desse...

Soprano Last Episode Farewell D...
June 10, 2007

Appetizers

Fresh Tomato Basil Bruschetta
Roasted Grilled Eggplant Bruschetta
Sauteed Polenta Rounds with Pesto
Battered Eggplant with Prosciutto;
Mozzarella, Tomato and Sage

Dinner

Italian Style Gravy served over Rigatoni
Meatballs, Sausage and Broccioli
Escarole and Arugula Salad with Asiago and Lemon Dressing

Dessert

Brownies and Chocolate Chip Cookies
Peach and Blueberry Compote over Icecream

Bone Appetitto!!!
Happy Birthday Steve!!!!

Tommy's Annual 47th Birthday Party

Appetizers

Mini Hot Dogs   Classic Onion Dip
Wild Mushroom Polenta with Fontina
Chicken Wings Savoy... Red Hot Wings
Peppercorn Tuna with Wasabi Sauce
Grilled Pork Tenderloin with Chic Peas and Red Seeds
Marinated Duck Breast with Scallion, Bell Pepper Vinaigrette
Smoke Salmon with Chives over Hot House Cucumbers
Fresh Mozzarella with Prosciutto, Baby Arugala and Roasted Peppers

Entrees

Lasagna Bolognese
Grilled London Broil with Essence of Port and Mushrooms
Hot and Sweet Sausage with Broccoli Ra...
Roasted Potatoes with Hot Peppers

Dessert

Super B...
Giants VS...
February 1...

Appetizers

Artichoke Dip   Onion Dip
Quesidallas with Fresh Gu...
Stromboli Rolls
Assorted Cheeses and Kick-O...
Spicy Chicken Wings

Main Cou...

New O...

Here is a list breakdown I use for a large party:

1 month ahead

Plan your menu!

Order invitations (if sending them)

Plan guest list to determine number of guests

Send out emails for save the date

Know your theme and plan accordingly

Rent any equipment you may need (i.e.: DJ, tent, tables, chairs, plates, glasses and hire any extra help you may need for bartending and clean up)

Start to purchase staple items (i.e.: jars or cans)

3 weeks ahead

Finalize your menu

Send out invitations or evites

Plan what make-aheads you will do and what can be frozen

Plan and purchase beverages, chill wine and any other refrigerated beverages

Make your shopping list

Start to purchase staple items and paper goods

Make or get name place cards ready

2 weeks ahead

Start to prepare anything that can be frozen (i.e.: cookies, cake layers, sauces and components of recipes such as pesto, etc.)

Order any specialty meats or flower arrangements

1 week ahead

Start to organize house and get rid of clutter

Clean all glassware, dishes and silverware you may be using

Iron tablecloths and set table

Type and print our your final menu and make adjustments later

Take out your platters, baskets and serving utensils. Start to label each piece with a sticky note with the food item on it. This will help you decide ahead of time how many platters, bowls and accessories you need. It's so helpful to your kitchen helpers so they know which food item goes on what with no confusion.

Clean out a front door closet for coats if rainy or cold

191

1 or 2 days ahead

Finish most of your perishable shopping

Finish your house and get everything in order. This is when I start to hide things and find them 3 months later!

Get your centerpieces and candles organized

Pick your playlist for great music

Check your set table and place name cards

Go over your checklist and cross off all that is done and ready

Defrost all items that were make-ahead in refrigerator

1 day ahead

Make sure your table is set and, if you have a buffet, that all your plates, napkins, utensils, etc. are all set

Finish centerpieces

Place a small flower vase and candle in bathrooms. It's welcoming and looks special. Stock with extra toilet paper, scented hand soap, decorative paper towels and hand creams that coordinate with the seasons.

Make sure dishwasher is empty

Get bar ready with wine glasses, wine opener and fruit garnishes (i.e.: lemons, limes, oranges, etc.)

Also, slice fruit for flavored water. Sliced cucumbers or lemons are favorites in our house and look pretty in glass pitchers. Try sliced citrus of any kind and/or sliced strawberries to make a lovely pink colored water for your party.

Buy ice if needed

Make sure all appropriate wine, beer, champagne and/or soda are all chilled if possible

Finish last minute perishable food shopping

Chop, blanch and mix anything that can last in the refrigerator before event and prep everything you possibly can

Wrap any baking or roasting pans for easy clean up in aluminum foil

Cut any finger desserts and have ready on tray in refrigerator

Day of party

Put ice in coolers and wine buckets. Chill all beverages.

Assemble platters and make any last minute items. Always wrap in plastic wrap and refrigerate until serving time.

Buy fresh bread if needed in the morning

Check menu to make sure you have everything

Frame the menu for display. This adds a nice touch to the table. Start saving your menus to cherish that moment in time around your table.

Have fun and enjoy your guests

Less is more

One of my dearest friends and talented photographers who photographed this book, Al Owens, taught me "Less is more." He said to keep food photography simple and not overdue it. I have used that concept in my entertaining and cooking as well. Try not to overthink your party and make it too complicated. I have always been a perfectionist but I found that people remember the food, fun, laughter and great time they have with family and friends—not if I garnished every one of my bruschetta toasts. Simplify and make a few ingredients sing in your dishes. It's not the quantity but the quality of each recipe's ingredients. Just a simple farm picked tomato with fresh mozzarella, a basil leaf and a drizzle of extra virgin olive oil will make your guests' mouthes water without lighting up your stove or oven. Keep it simple and easy while making everyone comfortable.

Maria's High School Graduation Party
June 21, 2008
GO HURRICANES!

Appetizers

Grilled Antipasto Platter with Mixed Veggies, Cheeses and Meats
South-West Medley with Fresh Guacamole, Tomato Salsa and Corn Relish with Cheese Quesadias
Middles Eastern Sampler with Minted Couscous, Eggplant Coppanata and Hummus.
Pepperoni Strombolis, Onion Dip, and Artichoke Dip
Herb and Lemon-infused Shrimp Cocktail

Entrees

Grilled Tex-mex style Steak Kabobs
Spicy Wingettes and Drumetts
Tricolor Sausage and Peppers
Grilled Hot ___ ___ie Pasta
Fresh ___
Arugula Salad with ___ ___, Peaches, and

Trico ___
Dilled ___
Fresh Tomato ___
Map ___
Grilled ___

Fresh Cann ___
Ice Cream ___

Alyssa's 50th Celebration
Appetizers

Grilled Tuna with Wasabi "White" Cream
Beef Fillet on Toast with Horseradish "White" Sauce
Smoked Salmon with Herbed "White" "Whip" Cream Cheese
Baked Polenta with "White" ___
Baked "White" Brie w___

Marisa's 12th Birthday Celebration!

Appetizers

Hot Artichoke Dip
Guacamole, Salsa and Sour Cream with Grilled Cheese Quesdillas
Eggplant Capanata with Hummus
Fresh Mozzarella with Tomato & Basil

Entrees

Marinated Baby back Ribs
Grilled Sausage and Peppers
Hot Dogs and Hamburgers
___ with Fresh Chives and Bacon
___rn Salad with Cilantro
___i-Color Cole Slaw
___asta Salad with Fresh Pesto
___ple Cured Baked Beans
___raut with Dijon and Apples

Dessert

Chocolate Banana Cream Birthday Cake
Chocolate Chip Cookie Cake
___-made Brownies   Fresh Fruit Salad
Icecream

MARISA'S TURNING ___
BIRTHDAY PAR___
JULY 6, 200___

APPETIZERS

SMOKED SALMON WITH DILL ___
ROASTED EGGPLANT AND H___
GRILLED QUESADILLAS WITH C___
BLACK BEAN ___
FRESH MOZZARELLA WITH ___
FRESH BRUSCHETTA WITH GRI___
ASSORTED DIPS AN___

DINNER ___

GRILLED HERBED CHICKEN ___
WITH PEPPERS AN___
GRILLED MARINATED STEAK SA___
GROWN BABY GREENS FROM UNCLE ST___
AUNT WENDI'S GARDEN
HOT DOGS AND HAMBURGE___
DILLED SHRIMP SALAD WITH MINI___
GRILLED CORN AND BARLE___
RED BLISS POTATO SALAD ___
CORN ON THE COBB BAKED B___

DESSERT ___

MARISA'S BLACK AND WHI___
STRAWBERRIES AND BAN___
CREAM ICECREAM CAK___
KNOTS___

Dinner With Friends
April 29, 2005

Appetizers

Skewered Antipasta Kebobs over Arugula
White Potato Pizza with Rosemary and Parmesan
Semolina Topped Hot Artichoke Dip
Sharon's Famous Brie

Main Course

Chicken Milanase with Yellow and Red Tomato Bruschetta with Ricotta Salada, Spinach and Portabella
Broccoli Rabe, Grilled Sausage and Cannellini Beans
Farfalle Pasta with Fresh Pesto and Grilled Roasted Tri-Color Peppers
Baby Green Salad with Goat Cheese, Endive, Dried Cranberry and Cinnamon Roasted Pecans with Raspberry/Fig Vinaigrette

Dessert

Lemon Curd Cheesecake   Chocolate Ganache Hazelnut Torte
Coconut Cream Pie   Cassis Drizzled Berry Fruit Compote
Black and White Chip Cookies

Dessert

Cannoli Filled Birthday Cake wit___
Triple Chocolate Brownies/
Fresh Summer ___

"Our Gang" BBQ Summer ___
July 19, 2014

Appetizers

Fresh Mozzarella with Jersey Beefsteak Tom___ and Basil
Bruschetta Topped with Sweetened Ricott___
Figs, Prosciutto and Honey
New Potato Pizza with Truffle Oil, Rose___
Parmesan Reggiano
Phyllo Encrusted Brie with Hot Pep___
Fresh Guacomole with Plaintain___

Main Course

Crostini with Tomato Coulis, Pesto & Olives

Baked Brie en Croute

Buffet Dinner

Batter Dipped Cutlets with Egg___
Balsamic Glaze, Port___
Grilled Pepper___
Toasted Orzo ___
Skewered Shrim___
Pear, Gorgonzola a___
Rosemary Por___

Dark White Chocolate ___
Raspberr___
Creme Anglaise goblet___
Fresh Fruit

Cappucino

Warmed Crabmeat ___
Brie Wrapped in P___
Grain ir___
Spinach Dip with ___
Onion Dip with C___

Kiddie Menu
Big Kids Menu
Honey Must___
meselun Gre___
Assorted ___
Roasted E___

Munch___
Cheese Platters
Dips   Pepperoni Stromboli
Salsa

Maria's 8th Birthday ___
Snacks

___ Onion Dip
___te with apricot Mustard
___ - cheddar & Ham
___ - pepperoni & mozzarella
Munchies

Main Course

Fajitas - Beef with Peppers, Lime Marinade
Chicken with Peppers, Lime Marinade
Accompaniements: Fresh Chunky Guacamole, Crisp Salsa,
Mexican Cheese Mix, Sour Cream
Spinach Salad with Fennel, mushroom & ___
with Raspberry Vinaigrette ___

Superbowl with
Appetizers

Ambience

Always create a warm atmosphere. Just lighting a candle, unscented if serving food, or a food-scented candle that goes with your menu, gives your guests a warm welcome as soon as they walk through the door. I also use simple flowers and prefer fruit, herbs and vegetables as my centerpieces by placing them in large glass vases with water in all different sizes. Just a simple vase filled with your favorite flower can turn a room into a special occasion. If I have surprise or last minute guests, sometimes I fill any glass container with whole or cut up fruit, a sprig of herbs or greenery I have outside, and I have a centerpiece. Also, don't forget your bathrooms. Add a small bud vase and a lighted votive candle for added charm.

We are from a musical family and have piano players, singers, dancers and musical theatre trained children. Our house would not be complete without great music. Pick your party playlist ahead of time and have it on when guests walk in. This gives the whole party a fun and relaxed atmosphere. The music can even pick up in tempo as the evening progresses.

People eat with their eyes

My food styling training and artful eye has made me love not only cooking, but also the art of food as well. When you serve and plate, just think about the texture, color and height of your placement. A spot of color goes a long way. For example, by adding a half of a cherry tomato on your dip with a sprig of parsley, your dip will go from ordinary to dazzling. Try and garnish with color and something that represents what is in the recipe. For example, if there is basil and lemon in the dip or salad, garnish with a bunch of basil leaves and slices of lemon. It will look beautiful and impress your guests.

Garnish suggestions

Savory items

> Lemons, limes and oranges: Sliced in wedges, slices, halves and/or zested with or without the leaves
> Herbs: Leaves of all kinds; rosemary sprigs, basil leaves, mint leaves, thyme, marjoram, oregano, lavender and chives with its blossoms are gorgeous.
> Fruit: Strawberries, raspberries, blueberries, grapes of all kinds and their leaves make beautiful lining for cheese platters.
> Olives of all kinds, pickles, roasted red peppers of all colors
> Chopped herbs and nuts
> Fruit leaves of all kinds (i.e.: lemons, oranges, grapes and figs)

Sweet items

> Chocolate shavings, chocolate curls
> Confectioner's sugar
> Cocoa powder
> Whipped cream
> Crystallized dried fruit

Place settings and cards

Mix old with new china, utensils, glassware and flatware

Make a place card for everyone

Preferred when everyone sits together, if they can, except for outdoor parties and buffets

In Appreciation

Thank you to my family whom I love beyond measure with all my heart, especially my husband Tom, and daughters, Maria and Marisa, for always believing in me. Thank you Tommy, my husband and best friend. Thank you for endlessly running around for specific, perfect ingredients (that may or may not have made you go crazy) and last minute shopping for every party, special occasion, shoot and this cookbook. Your patience, selfless love, laughter and kind heart gave me the calmness and strength to finish. I love you always and couldn't have done this without you.

My girls, Maria and Marisa, made me a bet to start my cookbook eight years ago and it came true! With their faith and endless support I had the confidence I needed to begin this book. I would never have had the courage to finish. Maria typed all the original recipes and Marisa proofread each one at the end, including all my copy, a multitude of times. My girls were my greatest inspiration and helped develop and test the recipes. They were my original taste tasters since they were babies. Their encouragement supercharged me with aspirations to follow my dream. They are my most precious blessings. I am so proud of them as they continue to shine in their own passions through all they do. Always believe, follow and listen to your heart with trust and ease. This is the path to true happiness. Share with the world your talents. Never, ever quit following your own dreams, my sweethearts. With faith and envisioning success all things are possible. I love you pumpkins with all my heart, always.

For my angels, Mom and Dad, who always believed in me and supported my passion. My Mom was my first assistant who tirelessly and lovingly helped me start my food career. We always had all the holidays and entertained constantly. My Mom taught me to get a party ready in no time with a moment's notice, and I loved doing it. That passion follows me to this day. My Dad guided me in all my career choices. My mentor, my advisor, my best friend, whom I try to emulate professionalism, a hard work ethic and determination from in all I do! He emphasized to do what you love and you will be great at it. His motto was to never quit and if you focus on what you believe in with faith, hard work and determination, anything is possible. They both encouraged me in every adventure I threw myself into and continue to encourage me in spirit in all I do. I love you both from here to heaven with all my heart.

For Michele Jerry and Al Owens, who inspired me with their incredible talents and unlimited creativity to make this book beautiful! I have been truly blessed with your friendships. Thank you, for your sincere support and many long but fun-filled days of photography at my house. It never feels like work when we are together. You were my informal taste testers for every recipe. Michele, your artful eye and gorgeous props made every recipe come to life. Your treasured friendship gave me the confidence to continue my goal. Dreams do come true! I could not have done this without you my precious friend. My Al, you are an incredible man and human being, and I will always look up to you on a pedestal as my adviser, mentor and cherished friend. Your wisdom and advice made this incredible journey a success. These gorgeous photographs brought my treasured food memories to life just the way I envisioned them. Your talent and creativity goes beyond the camera! My gratitude and love can not be measured! With laughter and tears you both were there for me every step of the way. Love you both beyond!

For Nancy Hourihan, how we were so blessed to meet by chance through my dear friend Christie Pagano. Thank you, Christie, for this wonderful gift. Nancy, thank you for my gorgeous cookbook design, artistic perfection on and off set and endless hours of putting the pieces together. Thank you beyond measure for your patience, talent and artistic magic. This is my showpiece. Love you dearly!

For Lisa Curran, who helped me with her artful eye and loving patience. I am so deeply grateful, love you!

For Devon Knight and Dave Katz for making me shine in my cookbook video. Your talents are beyond magical! Love you!

For Geovanna Colindres, who assisted in my kitchen for most of the book. Thank you for always knowing my next move in the kitchen and on set.

For Donna Saiewitz, who assisted in my kitchen and also tirelessly edited the first version of every one of my recipes with patience and precision. She also researched and created my index. Thank you Jack Hourihan for all of your help with the edits.

For Tracy McKenna, who came on board willingly to assist at the end of our shooting. You are magical and I'm so blessed you are in my life.

For my big sister Celeste, my confidante, who never stopped believing in me. She is the best cleaner-upper in the kitchen you will ever see. She is always here for me in any situation no matter how far away. I am forever grateful for all her endless trips to be by my side whenever I needed her. She is not only an amazing sister, but also my best friend. For her support and encouragement every step of the way, and for always making me feel so special in all I do. Love you, Big Sis.

For my Nana Daisy Pellicciotto, who taught me my first experiences in the kitchen growing up as a child. She was 90 going on 30! I hope to carry her youthful spirit always. The love and cooking traditions of my Italian family have inspired me my entire life. For my grandmother Maria Alia, who died at age 39 and I never met. I found out from my Dad that she contributed recipes to a food column in the *Guttenberg Gazette* during the late 1920's and early 1930's. I sense her being by my side as she inspires me, in spirit, with her love of food and tradition.

For my mother-in-law Elisa Malanga, who was an amazing cook. She shared her recipes lovingly and was always a terrific help to me in the kitchen for the holidays. She helped me tirelessly with my children, especially while I had to be on set day in and day out on particularly demanding jobs. She was a second Mom to me and I am eternally grateful for her love and support. I love you and miss you dearly. Her outstanding pizza will live on forever in our family. I did not know my father-in-law long, but he loved what I did for a living and always asked me a million questions about my shoots and recipes with a smile and a contagious, joyful Malanga laugh. His favorite was lemon meringue pie and I perfected my technique because of him. Love you with misses, Dad.

For my son-in-law Christopher McMahon. Thank you for eating everything that I make for you, even the whole leaves on the artichokes. It's a joy to feed you and I can't wait to cook numerous new memories together at our family table!

For Arthur Imperatore, Sr., Dad's best childhood friend and my inspiration in so many ways. We've enjoyed numerous talks for hours around my table while enjoying Sunday Gravy! Your keen sense of past history, propelling knowledge of our future, and insight have always resulted in positive advice for myself and my children that will last lifetimes. Thank you, Arthur, for being part of our family.

For my Cornell professors Marcia Pimentel, Dr. Gertrude Armbruster and Dr. Virginia Utermohlen. Your encouragement in my field through my studies and advice were invaluable. Thank you for inspiring my potential, keeping in touch and supporting my goals from the beginning. Cornell University will always be an important, vital and treasured part of my life.

For the amazing teachers and chefs at the New York Restaurant School and Le Cordon Bleu. Thank you for the intense culinary training that helped make me become the professional I am today.

For my food editor employers who gave me my first chance as a freelancer, William Rice at *Food & Wine*, Elizabeth Alston at *Woman's Day* and Jeanne Voltz at *Red Book*. I am deeply thankful for all I learned with you at the starting gate of my career path.

For Silvia Lehrer, for giving me my first job as your assistant at your cooking school, Cooktique, at age 16. This catapulted my culinary journey.

For my special colleagues Anna Marie Cesario, Marianne Arimenta and Vicky Hayes, who I met in the beginning of my career and became my closest, dearest friends. They have inspired, shared and taught me so much in their test kitchens, studios and homes. For their love of food and entertaining. Our conversations and world are always based on food. I will always cherish sharing ideas and recipes together, and our everlasting love and friendship. I love you all dearly!

For Deborah Ruggieri, Iggy Ruggieri and Sheila Wenke. You were an integral part of perfecting my career as a food stylist, on and off set. Our years on set helped me hone my skills, making me as proficient in the kitchen as I am in the studio. We learned so much together. Every job taught me something new while we discovered, created and had fun together all at the same time. Our careers brought us together but, most importantly, gave me lifelong, true friendships that I will treasure forever. Love you!

For Christina Nuzzo who took my portraits for this book. It was so truly me that I used it for this book. You are so talented.

For Justine Bylo for her professional and kind advise regarding self publishing.

For Ryan Brondolo, one of my son-in-law's dearest friends, who designed my Alysciouss logo. What a great gift that I love!

For my past and present assistants throughout my career. You all went beyond measure in making my job seamless while working so hard and always with a smile: Carmel Alia, Celeste Lafferty, Wendy Walters, Linda Cesario, Elisa Scarpino, Linda-Gail Alati, Fildelma Winters, Judy Gencarelli, Pattie Corrado, Helen Gabrysiak, Mary Jo Romano, Jackie Mercogliano, Sharon Carr, Geovanna Colindres, Vicky Hayes, Joanne Panayi, Linda Rivera, Donna Saiewitz, Russell Maitland, Tracy McKenna, Maria Malanga, Marisa Malanga, Christopher McMahon and Miriana Marqeuz.

For all my treasured food families, friends, chefs, photographers, art directors, assistants, agencies and graphic designers who have inspired me throughout my career in my craft of food styling, photography, cooking and art. Our experiences together shine through my work. Thank you for molding me into who I am today on and off the studio sets, kitchens, culinary schools and your homes. There are so many more people to thank I can't count but I wanted to especially thank the following people for all their kindness, sharing, teaching, opportunities, friendships and just for their love of food: Alia, Malanga, Lafferty, Pellicciotto, McMahon, Mercogliano & Merk families, Silvia Lehrer, Jacques Pepin, Giugliano Bugialli, Bruce Beck, Mrs. Betty Ann Maryott, Mrs. Kovak, Connie Fontana, Nancy Lenore, Peter Pioppo, Jerry Simpson, Gene Knowles, Dave Lewis, Donna Aristo, Tom Dilworth, Ysabel Martinez, Danisha Devor-Mackesey, Carol Ring, Terri Davis, Sharon Miller, Rick Becker, Ken Kephart, Lisa Curran, John Millington, Bill Truran, Dan Pitzczatoski ,Lou Manna, Andie Fazio, Nicole Kantanas, Carolyn Taylor, Jerry Errico, John Montana, Billy Arce, Pattie and Charles Corrado and family, Josephine DeAngelis, Dr. Linda Cesario, Joe Mazzo, Debbie Cesario, Daniel Cesario Jr., Linda Rivera and family, Marni Leslie, Lisa Kenny, Joanne Panayi, Diane Revels, Ceil Maher, Jackie Mercogliano, Sharon Carr, Tom, Sean, Nick and Chris Lafferty & family, Steve Adubato, Jr., Maria and Jack Panico, Diane Holtaway, Heather Bean, Lilia Temple, Mary Jo Romano, Les Herzog, Michele Harris, April Forman, Lisa DeStephano, Sean O'Brien, Sandy Cobin, Charlie Biondo, Joyce Lipinski Cascella, Janet Ellison Pearsall, Naomi Kettler, Jill Flack, Martha Garcia, Sheryl Abbot, James Smith, Jenna Smith, Faye Egan, Cathy Marschean-Spivak, Denise Casimono, Sarah Page, Dr. Mei Ling Imperatore, Dr. Rosalie Gagliardi, Maggie Smith, Diane Revels, Lauren Dellabella, Lisa Christiansen, Debbie, Ray, Renee & Janessa Celentano,Ruggieri family, Monaco Family, Scarpino Family, Cesario Family, Pagano Family, Alati Family, Donna Riccardi, Paul Gelsobello, Russell Maitland, Joe Wohlgemuth, Norma Jean Longfield, Carol Linger, Karen Deluca, Elizabeth Pelaez, Alan Stabile, Ybich Malanga, Justine Chapin, Lori Egan, Patty Mitchell, Julie Pham, Michelle Squillante, Susie Collier and My Gang (Doug Tanner, Bob Levai, Brain O'Connor, Dylan Craig, Artie Ley, George Mouakad, Nitza Goodman, Ernie Kolhsaat and Donna Galligan).

Just for the love it,

Alyssa xo

www.ingramcontent.com/pod-product-compliance
Lightning Source LLC
Chambersburg PA
CBHW040318100426

42811CB00012B/1477